From conflict containment
to resolution

The experiences of a
Moldovan–Northern Ireland self-help initiative

Michael Hall

in collaboration with

Joe Camplisson

Published June 2002 by Island Publications
132 Serpentine Road, Newtownabbey, Co. Antrim BT36 7JQ
Northern Ireland

ISBN: 1 899510 37 0

From conflict containment to resolution is an extended and updated
account of material originally published in the pamphlet
Hidden Frontiers (Island Publications, 1996)

This book was published with the generous financial assistance of
C S Mott Foundation, Flint, Michigan, USA

MICOM and the JCDC owe a debt of gratitude to so many people and
organisations – in Moldova/Transdniestria, Northern Ireland and elsewhere –
that it would be impossible to mention them all here; hopefully the inclusion of
some of their names within the book can serve as a token of appreciation.

The relationship between MICOM and its sources of funding has allowed both
to feel connected with areas of need and with each other. The success of this
relationship owes a special debt to: Ian Bell, formerly Charities Aid Foundation,
London; Jeanette Mansour, C S Mott Foundation, USA; Lord Hylton, House of
Lords, London; and the ways in which the UK Foreign and Commonwealth
Office, Westminster Foundation for Democracy, and Department for International
Development have responded.

MICOM is also grateful for the constant support and advice received over the
years from John W Burton, who became MICOM's patron in 2002.

Above all, a debt of gratitude is owed to all those from whom so much has been
drawn: the participants at MICOM/JCDC seminars, workshops and study visits
who not only gave their time so unselfishly, but spoke so honestly and eloquently
of their own experience of the threat which confronted them all – that of deep-
rooted, identity-related violent conflict.

Printed by Regency Press, Belfast

Contents

Introduction – the need for a new approach

Not only Islamic fundamentalists but many Western media commentators linked the rationale behind the appalling terrorist assault on the USA on 11 September 2001 – in which over 3000 innocent civilians perished – to, among other things, the unresolved Palestinian/Israeli conflict. Although the Palestinian Authority were quick to repudiate any such connection, there is no doubt that deep-rooted, identity-related conflicts such as that occurring in the Middle East provide terrorist groupings with a ready 'excuse' for their violence, and 11 September confirmed that some regional conflicts have global ramifications.

If the declaration of 'war on terrorism', however that is defined, is not complemented by a strenuous global effort to eradicate those injustices which sow the seeds of and sustain terrorism (inequality, poverty, economic exploitation and the denial of individual or national rights), and accompanied by a search for a radically new strategy for conflict resolution, then the world will *not* "have changed forever", as those commentators told us, but will doubtless witness many more such tragic days.

This book is concerned with this search for a new and more effective way of resolving deep-rooted, identity-related violent conflict – and by that is meant conflict where there is a strong element of ethnic, religious or cultural enmity, although experience has revealed that the conflict resolution process described in these pages might have a relevance well beyond such categories.

The narrative describes the efforts of a Belfast-based organisation, MICOM (Moldovan Initiative Committee of Management) to assist in the creation of a new and democratic society for the peoples of Moldova and its breakaway region of Transdniestria, and to help engender movement towards a meaningful resolution of their destabilising, self-destructive, albeit frozen conflict.

The Director of MICOM and his closest associates are, in the main, ordinary citizens who, when confronted by the spiralling inter-communal violence which engulfed Northern Ireland from 1969 onwards, were forced to acquire an expertise in community development and conflict resolution skills. In 1991, while working in the Balkans, MICOM's Director received requests from individuals in Moldova to focus these skills on the Moldovan/ Transdniestrian conflict, acting as an 'external third party'. The process which MICOM helped initiate soon led to the birth of a local partner in Moldova, the JCDC (Joint Committee for Democratisation and Conciliation). Like MICOM, the members of the JCDC are ordinary citizens who, realising that their respective political leaderships were unable to resolve their conflict or effectively address severe socio-economic deprivation, came together from both sides of that conflict in a self-help attempt at addressing their needs. The JCDC, through its commitment and effort, was soon able to act in Moldova as an 'indigenous third party'.

As the narrative unfolds the reader will see how the MICOM/JCDC partnership has been able to engage with all levels of leadership within Moldova and Transdniestria in an often complex, but always productive, conflict resolution process, which is itself an integral part of an overarching community development strategy. Village mayors, parliamentarians, high-ranking political leaders and a plethora of NGOs (non-governmental organisations) have been brought into the process. The Northern Ireland connection has also been utilised to the full, with various exchange visits attempting to share experiences and stimulate movement. Furthermore, this integrated conflict resolution/community development process has proven itself able, to the surprise of many in the field of conflict resolution, to work closely and effectively alongside a separately introduced, international mediation process in Moldova led by the OSCE.

Hopefully this book will prove of value to all those with an interest in conflict resolution theory and practice, whether as scholar-practitioners working in the field, or as communities who suddenly find themselves caught up in those tragic situations where neighbour turns upon neighbour. To assist scholar-practitioners and communities alike, the narrative is concerned not merely with the theoretical underpinnings of the process of conflict resolution but with its *practicalities*, dealing with such questions as:

- what was actually discussed at seminars and workshops?
- what were the problems which were identified?
- how were different levels of leadership brought into a shared approach to tackling these problems?
- what methods did the facilitators utilise?

Such detail is included in the hope that it may prove of value to those confronting conflict situations. There is an unfortunate tendency for some to attempt to shroud their profession in an aura of mystery. This book reveals the commonsense realities of conflict resolution, so that those who find themselves caught up in circumstances of conflict will not be left bewildered and helpless, but will know how conflict-related needs may be satisfactorily addressed and how momentum towards resolution can be engendered.

Michael Hall

Part 1

The Moldovan Initiative

erg
dis
the con

Av
Crea

In N
pitted t
them
of po

of Yugoslavia.

In late 1969, the
of a mixed Catholic/Protestant, non-g
Relations C
development strate
and disaffection be
was Joe Campli
when the housg
interface
employment
communit
common
Nickt
had come to
only assist local c
could also be

The N'C
forerunner of
that with Catholi

...rv...es...to...r...hour Burton, a leading world specialist in conflict resolution. His base of... work the... on what he called his 'Basic Human Needs Theory'.

Not long after his start, Camplisson was impressed by Burton's demonstrations of his approach. In particular, when he... both... a top paramilitary leader (from the O... d IRA) and some of his associates into a 'problem solving' process, examining their own and their enemy's positions. This process helped reveal that: the conflict they and their adversaries were engaged in had an illusory character, an... an... coherence to the military option was a self-defeating strategy; they had a problem to be solved rather than an enemy to be destroyed. Burton believed that this *assisted analysis*, the quintessential element in the problem-solving process, could bring adversaries to a 'win-win' outcome which would see... their respective identity need satisfiers.

To Camplisson here was a new language which challenged the standard approach which had dominated the field of conflict resolution up to then: that of mediated negotiation, with its reliance on confrontational, adversarial, power-bargaining. Burton's problem-solving approach sounded utopian but the new language... a perceived truth once the nature and manner of this form of assisted analysis most likely made sense to that paramilitary leader as he subsequently... led... his organisation into a unilateral ceasefire... tion

... by 19... C... on had no inkling of the important contribution made by... in the... time. Years later Camplisson himself would find Burton's theories helpful to him in his own attempts to assist in the resolution of another bitter, long... conflict at the other edge of Europe.

John Burton (left) and Joe Camplisson, while attending a ... at The University of Ljubljana, 1996.

10

Moldova and Ireland: the troubled fringes of Europe

When television alerted the world to the appalling plight of Romania's orphans – following the downfall of the Ceausescu regime in 1989, the year which saw Communism collapse throughout Eastern Europe – many people in Northern Ireland felt a desire to respond. In Belfast, much of this energy was channelled through the network of community organisations which had sprung up throughout working-class areas from 1969 onwards as 'The Troubles' enveloped and communities attempted to counteract the effects of the ongoing violence.

In the Ainsworth area of Belfast's Shankill Road residents began to bring groceries and clothing to Ainsworth Community Centre, asking its leading community worker, Louis West, if these could be sent to Romania. West approached Farset, the community development project, to see if its vehicles could be utilised. Jackie Hewitt, Farset's manager, had already been giving the matter serious consideration:

> Our Chairman, Rev. Roy Magee, had recently been out to Romania and had returned quite devastated by what he had seen. I was becoming [illegible] ... So in 199[illegible] we decided [illegible] put together a proposal [illegible] ground in a more structured way.

Among [illegible] community development specialist [illegible]. Since the demise of the Northern Ireland Community Relations Commission he had worked independently through his [illegible] Community Development Services. [illegible] Romania's [illegible] grassroots [illegible] the [illegible] [illegible] local government [illegible] counterparts [illegible] Northern Ireland [illegible] Romania [illegible] programme for [illegible] the physically [illegible]

[illegible]

most [illegible]
which included the [illegible]
principally [illegible] in Romania [illegible]
the [illegible] Soviet Socialist Republics [illegible]

... to border between Moldova and ... on the foreign jurisdictions. When Romania ... moved into the city, this was seen by ... that Russia's president, Boris ... settle and stop the bloodshed". ... gradually President Snegur of Moldova ... administration was accorded special ... were ... (in place later). The ... in the event of ... Russian, Moldovan and Transdniestrian ... placed ... the region to monitor the ceasefire.

ROMANIA

MOLDOVA

REPUBLIC of MOLDOVA (including Transnistria)
Major ethnic groups: Moldovan (64%), Ukrainian
Economy: Wine, tobacco, food-canning
Physical: Landlocked area consisting of hilly plains with

We currently ... ...

It was ... if Campbell ... ... it was clear evidence ... ... just was to be a major ... ... which he was ... admitted.

The wish to the south ... ... took a warm display of camaraderie ... ... police ... ... resolution. Many ... ... associates, Grigorg ... ... Office in Chisinau ... ... extended heavy fighting ... ... police station ... ... Across the road ... ... which ... ... tanks had ... ... Moldovan ... ... keeping force was in place ... ... again.

Campbell ... ... chief of police and the Russian ... ... in charge of the peace-keeping ... ... the military ... ... to sit in the company of the police ... ... chief offered Campbell ... ... movement ... here which could take ... ... son then met separately with the ... ... be just as hospitable and just as willing to ...

With the goodwill ... ... of the Joint Control Commission ... ... force. He too wanted to be ... ... Campbell ... ... the new leader of the breakaway Transdniestria ... ... had the ultimate authority to take a ... ... travelled to Tiraspol and was ... ... it in a process ... ... help with the resolution of the conflict ... ... engage in work anywhere in ... industry. A ... ... from the Moldovan leader, President She ... was ... ... following ...

Campbell also ... ... with the conflict resolution process ... ... which ... ... in the search for solutions – Russia, ... that would int...d

...commi...ee
... ...ess of the
... ...estr...
...odices... ...ta...
...th...n...d...y...ours
...ut ...ae ex-prison... Tommy
...er... ...unity Dev...lopment
...d... ...in...ted ...l...rly th... th...
situation ... ...p...s...t in Northern I...land in
1...9... ... ...ch ... T... ...h...... ...inject a sense of
urge...y ...ee...

Th... ...mm... be ...d th... N... ... ...nfere...res, with its mem...
drawn ...g... ...n ho... d... ...nd ...rans...i...ri..., f...rmalised itself int...
what we... ...ne ...... s t... ... ...e Committee for Democratisation and
Concili... ...i, ...bl... ...n go beyond its initial task of
organi... ...rt... ...e lead facilitator in the community
devel... ... ...or...ing to be a powerful dynamic within the
process...

There ... ...hi...
Campi... ... ...i...ly, the
comm... ... ...nferen...s.
Secon... ... ...ved to assist in
bring... ... ...p...... ...t...y
to en...... ...p...... ...wo...l...require the
e...nt...

✝ ...

♣ ...

Faced with such a daunting programme Camplisson set about gathering expert support. As a result of his work in Northern Ireland, he had become a Distinguished Fellow of the Centre for Conflict Analysis and Resolution at George Mason University, Virginia, USA, and he contacted its Director, Chris Mitchell, for assistance. He also contacted his former mentor John Burton, who was now retired and living in Australia. Burton suggested that Camplisson approach John Groom, Professor of International Relations at the University of Kent in Canterbury. Burton and Groom had worked together in the past and had set up the Centre for Conflict Analysis at Kent.

Groom arranged for experts in international relations to participate in studies at the London School of Economics (LSE), during which Camplisson's proposals were assessed, challenged and supported. Some of these experts expressed an interest in being more closely involved and a 'support team'[†] formed: Jonathan Cohen, John Groom, Mark Hoffman, Vivienne Jabri, Chris Mitchell, Norbert Ropers, Irene Sage, Keith Webb and Andy Williams.

A wider interest in the process was also growing. In May 1994, Mark Hoffman, LSE, arranged for Camplisson to deliver a paper, in Kiev, on his work to Ukrainian defence chiefs, government officials, academics and NATO officials. NATO's participation, unthinkable only a few years before, was made possible because of the 'Partnership for Peace' entered into by NATO and the nations of the former Soviet Bloc.

The tragic events in the former Yugoslavia lent an added urgency to conflict resolution efforts in Moldova at the other side of the Balkans. As in Yugoslavia there were no neat dividing lines between the various ethnic communities and on either side of the conflict interface the different population groups lived side by side – any renewal of inter-communal violence could see a Yugoslav-type 'ethnic cleansing' spiral out of control.

The JCDC succeeded in bringing together the participants who had attended the first two Nitra conferences for a third, joint conference, held in June 1994. Two groups of 44 delegates, one from each side of the Moldovan conflict, met with foreign experts in the fields of agronomy, economic development, community development, international relations, conflict analysis, civil policing, journalism and the voluntary sector. Facilitators were drawn from the United Kingdom, the United States, Canada, Germany, Romania and Russia.

However, while there was some continuity, in that Nitra III included participants who had attended either Nitra I or Nitra II, there were many new faces who were not familiar with what was being attempted. This, coupled with inadequate preparation, almost undermined the whole process.

Some of these new faces came expecting to address political needs directly related to the conflict. They wanted to put forward resolutions espousing their

---

† This relationship proved invaluable and continued until 1997.

cause and when they found the other delegates discussing the needs of a collective farm or river pollution they were thrown off-balance. A small group from the 'Latin' side, who would have been among the supporters of unification with Romania and who were unhappy with the more pragmatic stance then being pursued by Moldova's political leaders,† suspected that the conference had a hidden, government-inspired agenda. Even when it was presented to them as merely a study/workshop, the purpose of which was to assist self-help action, the suspicions of this minority were not assuaged.

Matters came to a head when they stormed the stage and made fiery speeches for some fifteen minutes. It was a tense experience for Camplisson and the facilitators. Eventually, however, the microphone was given back and Camplisson attempted to re-focus the proceedings to meet community development requirements, against a background of simmering tensions. These tensions surfaced again in the workshops despite the efforts of the facilitators, who, while experts in their own fields, had little experience or training in handling such situations. Throughout the workshops and immediately afterwards it was clear that the disaffected minority were attempting to convince the other Moldovan delegates to withdraw completely.

Assistance came, however, from an unlikely quarter. NATO had originally intended to send a representative but when he was unable to attend due to illness they suggested that Camplisson invite a Romanian journalist who had been a leading figure in Radio Free Europe and was then living in Germany. He accepted the invitation and with his Romanian background and pro-Western bias he was seen by the dissidents as someone sympathetic to their cause. But he himself could see that what they were engaged in was folly and so he and a colleague worked patiently behind the scenes in an attempt to reassure the most vocal of the dissidents that there was no covert political agenda being pursued. Through this intervention and the renewed efforts of the facilitators the dissidents finally accepted that Nitra III was not a high-powered political debating forum which could solve the Moldovan crisis, but purely an attempt at personal, organisational and process development, related to shared needs. It had been a close-run thing, but the conference had been saved, with many ideas for social, economic, cultural and political advancement, including action plans – many of them joint plans – being taken back to villages, towns and cities on each side.

---

† In the late 1980s the success of the pro-Romanian Popular Front of Moldova (PFM) had seemed to indicate a swift Moldovan unification with Romania. However, despite large demonstrations in support of PFM demands, the reality, both at community and at political level, was more complex. Opinion polls carried out after 1989 demonstrated little support for a union with Romania among the population in general, and there was increasing evidence that the Republic's majority population considered themselves Moldovan rather than Romanian. The result of the Moldovan parliamentary election of February 1994 (which gave a majority to those parties committed to Moldovan independence rather than unification with Romania) was further evidence of this reality.

Enter the political leaderships

The Moldovan leader, President Snegur, and the Transdniestrian leader, President Smirnov, had followed Camplisson's efforts with interest, in keeping with their requests for assistance. Under the auspices of the Conference for Security and Co-operation In Europe (CSCE), which had set up a peace mission in Moldova in April 1993, the two governments had established 'Expert Groups', charged with devising suitable constitutional arrangements which would assist a settlement of the conflict. The governmental representatives involved in the CSCE-mediated negotiations also represented their governments in the conflict resolution process. The challenge for Camplisson was how to engage these two Expert Groups in a conflict resolution process which would be compatible with the CSCE-mediated negotiation process. The conflict resolution process – a process of analysis – would use the 'Transdniestrian issue' to push the analysis towards its root causes. The process of negotiations, however, would endeavour to bring the two parties to accept a compromise political settlement. Each process, therefore, had the potential to frustrate the other. Camplisson also realised that a conflict resolution process engaging the political leaderships would require a different approach from that used at Nitra:

> In a conflict situation ordinary people do not have the capacity, the responsibility or the authority to deliver resolution. It is only those in political, military or even paramilitary leadership who are in a position to initiate meaningful movement towards a settlement. These two groupings, then, have different needs and must be engaged in different ways.
>
> For those at the grassroots struggling to survive from day to day you endeavour to help them address their needs in ways which bring them into productive relationships with perceived adversaries, in the hope that mutual benefit is derived at both the personal and the community level. This was the purpose behind the Nitra-type conference/workshops.
>
> For the political leaders, however, the *reverse* is the case. While you obviously want to establish sufficient trust to permit a working partnership, you are *not* concerned with building interpersonal relationships between the opposing leaders – this is to be avoided. As the political leaders are the only ones with authority to resolve the conflict, you want to *hold them* to a representation of the extreme positions as they bring their constituencies towards a 'win-win' outcome. It would be pointless if opposing leaders became 'buddies' and no longer accurately represented the fears and aspirations which gave rise to the conflict within their respective communities. Such leaders would undoubtedly experience 're-entry' problems when they returned to those communities, and might even be replaced by others felt to be more representative of the extremes, with the result that the credibility of the process would be destroyed.

It was now that Camplisson recalled the lessons he had learned from John Burton's conflict resolution work in Northern Ireland:

> One of Burton's ideas which I was drawn to was that of trying to get people into a situation where, with the help of a third party, they could judge whether or not what they were doing was self-defeating. There was no point in *me* telling them that, they had to be placed in a position where they could set out their objectives, evaluate their strategy for achieving those objectives, and then determine *for themselves* whether it was taking them towards those objectives or taking them further away. Even if they didn't start out with any clear objectives, you could still focus on motivations, even negatively expressed ones – "I want the Brits out" or "I want the IRA destroyed" – and help them look beyond such statements and determine what fears or aspirations they reflected.
>
> Another of Burton's assumptions which I share is that it is those on the extremes who feel most acutely the problem which exists. The steadfastness of belief which is often a feature of extremism allows extremists to truly represent that which has given rise to the conflict – and it is *through them that you can get sight of the problem*. Of course, when you start to work with the extremes, assisting a self-analysis of their positions, it needs to be done not in isolation but within a process, so that both sides can see how their respective positions have evolved and been influenced by the *other* side. Often it boils down to significant identity needs, which are not necessarily expressed through political, social or economic issues, but through the symbols which people want to have in place. So the question becomes one of how they can pursue identity needs satisfaction yet avoid coming into conflict with those whose security of identity is perceived to be threatened by such pursuit.
>
> The process which brings them to that point unfolds while they are sitting across the table from one another, and Burton's conflict resolution theory holds that people can only ultimately satisfy their *own* needs by recognising that the needs of the enemy have also to be met, and that *they* too have something to say in satisfying the needs of their enemy.

As a first step, senior representatives of both governments were brought to a workshop at the University of Kent, Canterbury, in July 1994. This was conducted by Camplisson; John Groom, University of Kent; and Chris Mitchell, George Mason University. Camplisson need not have worried about the two delegations becoming 'buddies'. They refused to travel together, insisted on coming in different planes and on staying in different hotels.

The workshop soon threw up dilemmas for the organisers. Camplisson had explained to the two Presidents that the encounter would be handled using a 'problem-solving' process. However, the two delegations assumed that this meant they should throw onto the table 'problems' such as customs, currency, the army and similar matters. These issues, Camplisson believed, should be used to push the analysis. Settlement of these issues would be helpful in *containing* the conflict, but not *resolving* it. To him, a 'problem-solving' approach was analytical. The first stage of this analysis (the 'mapping out of the conflict') involved the different protagonists determining the *nature* of the conflict, *who* was involved in it and who therefore had to be engaged in the search for solutions. Then they had to have a clear, shared understanding of their own and each other's positions within the conflict, a shared assessment of options (including military) for remedy and what sort of mechanisms were necessary for movement towards resolution. The alternative was that the two sides might indeed agree to some 'political settlement' yet continue to regard each other as enemies to be destroyed, so that while the conflict might be temporarily contained *it would not have disappeared*. The need, therefore, was for the adversaries to redefine their conflict as a 'problem to be solved', and keep redefining it until its true nature was clarified. Although this dilemma was not resolved at Canterbury the workshop was nevertheless viewed positively by the two governments.

With the work being undertaken in Moldova becoming increasingly complex, the Moldovan Initiative Committee of Management (MICOM) was established, with Camplisson as its Executive Director and Canadian Irene Sage its Deputy Director. Lord Hylton, a campaigner on penal affairs and human rights with a long interest in Northern Ireland, became MICOM's chairman. Also on the MICOM Executive was Ian Bell, Charities Aid Foundation.

Among academic colleagues offering support was American Mark Hoffman, lecturer at the LSE and a specialist in conflict resolution and international relations. He was to become a core member of the conflict resolution team which would gradually emerge. The JCDC was represented on MICOM's Executive by its chairman, Yuri Ataman, and Evghenii Berdnikov.

Camplisson also had the support of colleagues in Belfast, such as management consultant and President of Farset Barney McCaughey, and community activist and pamphleteer Michael Hall. Just as importantly, the C S Mott Foundation, Michigan, USA, had learned of Camplisson's efforts and had offered to provide core funding – prior to this his efforts had been unsalaried.

A second workshop was planned for January 1995. However, a political impasse had since developed, with the two sides in Moldova refusing to meet and the international intermediaries having no success in bringing them together. Nevertheless, because MICOM was accepted as a non-governmental organisation with no hidden agenda, both sides agreed to participate.

The dilemma which had arisen at the first Canterbury conference surfaced again at the second one – day-to-day political needs dominated the proceedings, consigning any problem-solving approach aimed at conflict resolution to the background. Camplisson and his associates realised that the two components – the immediate political needs and the longer-term conflict resolution needs – had to be married in some way, even if this was something of a retreat, for a failure to address immediate needs could be detrimental to the process. Accordingly, he introduced an exercise used at one of the Nitra conferences:

> At the end of the first day's session everyone was given a handful of blank cards to take back to their hotel room. On these cards they were each asked to write down suggestions relating to the following four categories: what they felt *their side* might do to move things towards resolution; what they felt the *other side* might do; what they thought they could *do together*; and finally what they thought the *international community* could do. After they left I was quite apprehensive, for I realised I was asking them all to make individual judgements and yet these people came from an authoritarian political culture where it was only those at the very top who took such decisions. The next morning could have been the end of my role in the process and it was with great relief that I saw them coming back with all their cards completed.

In fact, the exercise produced dozens of different issues. This opened up some very productive discussions among the two teams of delegates and many of those issues were incorporated into Presidential agreements which subsequently evolved (some of which, however, have still to be ratified).

The outcome of the conference was acclaimed by the two presidents and was welcomed by President Yeltsin's permanent representative in Moldova, Ambassador Vassev. The intergovernmental conflict resolution process launched at Canterbury also gained the active support of the Head of the OSCE[†] peace mission in Moldova, who lauded the Canterbury outcomes.[††]

The American Ambassador to Moldova, Mary Pendleton, later expressed her enthusiasm to Camplisson, saying that the conflict resolution process was helping to "rearrange the protagonists' mental furniture". The process had also helped to engender a shift in American perceptions. Prior to Canterbury II the Americans would not deal with the Transdniestrians because as a 'breakaway' region they were still an illegal entity, but now they revealed a preparedness to look at Transdniestrian needs as well.

In June 1995, at the request of the State Secretary of Transdniestria and the Department of Foreign Affairs, Moldova, Camplisson visited Moldova with Lord Hylton and Mark Hoffman, in part to assist the two governmental Expert Groups prepare for a summit meeting of their presidents. A few days later, at the invitation of President Snegur of Moldova and President Smirnov of Transdniestria, Camplisson attended this summit meeting, thereby raising the conflict resolution process to the highest political level.

[†] In 1994 the CSCE changed its name to the OSCE (Organisation for Security and Co-operation in Europe).

[††] The Expert Groups engaged in a third conflict resolution workshop at Canterbury in September 1996, with the international Mediators present solely as observers. This arrangement failed in practice and neither process was advanced. Camplisson and Hoffman, however, drew lessons from this failure and realised that a more effective complementarity between the two processes had to be established. This was also the final workshop held at Canterbury; all subsequent MICOM-assisted attempts at conflict resolution were to take place in Moldova, Northern Ireland or Bulgaria.

Community in its many dimensions

Community-based self-help action launched by the Nitra conferences had not remained static while the political leaderships were being engaged in the separate, but complementary, conflict resolution process. MICOM's local partner in Moldova, the JCDC, had been facilitating community development initiatives in cities, towns and villages. In order to assist the growth and strengthening of the JCDC, both as individuals and as a group, MICOM felt it would be valuable to engage them in a comparative study with individuals and groups working with similar problems in Northern Ireland.

In August 1995 members of the JCDC came to Belfast. Their programme included placements which complemented the visitors' diverse occupational backgrounds. Towards the end of their stay they were brought together for two days of workshops with local community activists, equally representative of their own divided society. The purpose was to afford the participants an opportunity to draw lessons from one another's experiences, and to assist movement towards the resolution of their respective conflicts.

The discussions which ensued during the exploration of their two conflicts – and the two 'versions' of each of those conflicts – did throw up clear parallels. Each conflict had been preceded by a phase during which any identity-related tensions appeared dormant and it was social and economic needs which predominated. Then some catalyst acted to disturb this: in Moldova it was the period of *glasnost* and the demands for civil liberties; in Northern Ireland it was the demands made by the Civil Rights movement. When such demands encountered structural resistance within the respective political systems the purely 'civil rights' issues were quickly overtaken by the reawakening of identity-related tensions, which in turn had led to an escalating violence.

There was a consensus within the workshops that violence had been totally counterproductive. One of the Moldovan delegation summed up his feelings:

> What was the outcome for us? Moldova lost the chance to build a new, united and independent republic. Because of the mistrust created between people in both areas and between all the different nationalities, we ended up instead with economic chaos and increased criminality. Many people regret what happened and are trying to rebuild that trust and find a solution.

One of the Northern Irish participants expressed a similar conclusion:

> Our experiences have led some of us to believe that the future has to be an *agreed* one – we cannot end up with a reluctant or rebellious minority, no matter which community forms that minority.

Camplisson pointed out one fundamental lesson to be drawn from the Moldovan conflict – that both government and people there were engaged in movement towards conflict resolution and had decided not to seek a 'victory', a situation which had not yet developed in Northern Ireland where people were a long way from accepting the idea of a 'win-win' outcome.

Although the workshops did not set out to determine how the two conflicts could be resolved, various pointers emerged as important in facilitating movement towards such resolution. Barney McCaughey summarised them as follows:

- There was a need to have (conflict resolution) work proceeding at *all* levels, whether individual, local community or governmental.
- There was a need to ensure that these levels worked in a complementary fashion.
- There was the need to ensure that one or more levels remained functioning even if others were stalling or had failed.
- Legitimate civil rights grievances had to be addressed.
- No-one should be excluded from the process, for those denied the opportunity to use the 'force of argument' more readily resorted to the 'argument of force'.
- An infrastructure had to be developed which would enable groups to meet and enter into dialogue with one another.
- Not all differences of perception or historical interpretation could be resolved, so time should not be wasted striving for agreement on every divisive issue.
- It was important to identify issues on which people *could* talk and work together, such as community development issues. This would help in the building of trust and relationships.
- Disagreeing with one's opponents did not mean refusing to *listen* to them.
- The raising of community awareness was an integral part of the process, as well as trying to encourage the media to promote its positive side.

The aspect of the exchange with most significance for the JCDC was the realisation that community groups in Northern Ireland were able to work together on a wide variety of issues *irrespective* of whether their society's conflict was on its way to resolution or not, and that in such co-operation there was no requirement that people in either community need abandon or dilute their deepest aspirations. The example this presented to the JCDC was to have almost immediate impact.

Along the Dniester river two adjoining towns shared a common industry. One town, Rezina, possessed a large quarry from which the raw materials were unearthed which were used in the manufacture of cement. The cement factory was located in the other town, Rybnitsa. There was a major problem, however: Rezina lay on the west (Moldovan) bank of the river, while Rybnitsa lay on the east (Transdniestrian) bank. During the fighting of 1992 all commerce and contact between the two jurisdictions ceased, leaving the citizens of each town to eye each other warily, while the overhead cable system used to transport buckets of raw material across the river lay idle. 1,400 workers in both the quarry and the cement works, and all peripheral service industries, became instantly unemployed.

Once the ceasefire came into effect a few individuals began to ask whether co-operation between the towns could be resurrected. However, each town was now using its own currency, there was a new customs post between them, cross-river movement was difficult, and the political atmosphere on both sides did not encourage any link-up between them at that time. Given such obstacles, no real co-operation was deemed possible.

The ex-mayor of Rybnitsa, Evghenii Berdnikov, was a member of the JCDC delegation to Belfast. Inspired by the evidence they had seen there of inter-community co-operation, he and the other members of the JCDC decided to proceed boldly. Despite encountering criticism and suspicion from both sides, within a few weeks of returning to Moldova they had managed to bring representatives of the two towns together. Camplisson was contacted and asked to chair the first meeting – using him as a necessary figurehead to deflect any possible criticisms aimed at either side. That meeting was extremely successful and the two sets of local representatives agreed to co-operate across a wide range of issues. Berdnikov publicly attributed the impetus behind the venture directly to the Northern Ireland exchange. And, of course, one of the first initiatives which they agreed would help break down some of the barriers preventing economic co-operation was only too obvious – the resumption of contact between the quarry and the cement works.

A workshop in Belfast. From left: Yuri Ataman (JCDC); Irina Colina (JCDC); Mark Hoffman (LSE) *standing*, Tommy Gorman (Springfield Inter-Community Development Project).

Moldovan conflict resolution process moves to Northern Ireland

On a field trip to Moldova in October 1995, Camplisson found that the governmental Expert Groups were locked into yet another impasse and that even the OSCE could not inveigle them to re-enter dialogue. However, when Camplisson met with the two sides, they both intimated that *he* might bring them together.

To their surprise, Camplisson informed them that he did not consider this would be useful. He realised intuitively that these recurrent impasses were symptomatic of a much deeper problem, namely that the *roots of the conflict* between the two sides were not being fundamentally addressed. Therefore, as long as these deep antagonisms remained unresolved, any mediated negotiations, with the expectation upon both sides to make progress, only served to threaten them, forcing them to retreat.

> I realised that they needed to step back from things and examine them, and prepare themselves for going forward into a third-party assisted process of conflict resolution. I suggested that they needed new insights into how to deal with their conflict and that one way to do this might be through a 'study visit' to Belfast. I fully understood that they had the responsibility to find constitutional arrangements which would allow them to function and survive, and this is what the OSCE was facilitating. Our role, MICOM's role, however, was different – it was to help them, through assisted analysis, to deal with the complexities of the *underlying* conflict between them and their role within that conflict.

Both sides agreed and a study visit to Belfast took place in March 1996 (by this time the impasse had been broken but the Expert Groups felt that the purpose of the visit remained valid). In his welcoming remarks to the two governmental delegations, the assembled facilitators and the Northern Irish participants, Camplisson set out his hopes for the exchange:

> In many respects you in Moldova are far ahead of us on the path to conflict resolution. You have already accepted that there is a *problem to be solved*. You have moved away from the notion – one that we retain here in Northern Ireland – that the *other person* is the problem. You have also accepted the need for a 'win-win' outcome for both parties. You have reached, if you like, the 'starting blocks' of a conflict resolution process – you have agreed to approach this in a 'problem-solving' way.

Camplisson's assertion that the visitors had already embarked upon a genuine conflict resolution process seemed to be borne out by the introductory remarks made by a spokesman for the Moldovan delegation:

I think it would be right to go into the roots of our conflict without blaming each other, without seeking the culprit. We are still far away from an agreement, but we should not be too hasty – step by step we will be able to solve the problem.

For their part, the Transdniestrian delegation echoed the same sentiments, reiterating that "violence is not a solution".

Some similarities between the Northern Ireland and Moldovan conflicts had already been highlighted during the 1995 community-level exchange; in particular, the fact that political alignments in both countries tended to be identity-related. A Northern Ireland/Moldovan encounter, therefore, had the potential to highlight important lessons for decision-makers in each conflict. As the Northern Ireland conflict was still far from resolution after a quarter of a century, an insight into why this was so could serve as a lesson – and, indeed, a warning – to the Moldovans. Conversely, as the parties to the Moldovan conflict had embarked upon a genuine conflict resolution process only four years after full-scale civil war, a insight into why and how this had come about could serve as a lesson to the Northern Irish.

As the then-current Northern Ireland conflict, notwithstanding its centuries-old character, owed its genesis to decisions and actions undertaken by all sides – government and opposition – in the late 1960s and early 1970s, the organisers of the exchange decided to set their focus there, and to bring many of the key players of that period into a retrospective analysis of their policies, strategies and tactics. The organising committee – Rev. Roy Magee, a Presbyterian minister who had helped broker the Loyalist ceasefire of October 1994; Paul Arthur, a professor of politics who had been involved in the Civil Rights movement; and Camplisson – had the capacity to identify such leaders and persuade them to participate, and those identified willingly did so, even in the knowledge that they would not find it easy to sit alongside those whom they still perceived as 'the enemy'. The intention was to determine, aided by hindsight, to what extent the policies and tactics of these players had been self-defeating, when measured against their original aspirations and objectives.

Having been preceded by a lecture by Jonathan Bardon on Irish history which set the Northern Ireland conflict in its broader European dimension, the workshops opened with a presentation by Harry West, former Northern Ireland government minister, who gave his analysis of how the ruling Unionist Party had viewed the descent into violence. In his opinion the Northern Ireland government had "brought immense prosperity to all shades of opinion in the country" but was unable to appease "the minority within the minority whose overall ambition was to destroy the state". Despite the introduction of a package of reforms which dealt with the main Civil Rights demands, IRA violence had persisted and could only have been defeated by resolute action by the British government. Not only was this not forthcoming but the British Prime Minister Edward Heath effectively halted the democratic process by closing down the Northern Ireland Parliament.

West was followed by Paul Arthur who felt that Northern Ireland had been "a society without empathy, where we had no understanding of the other side". Unionist distrust of the 'disloyal' minority, coupled with the minority's own feeling of being oppressed, combined to create the mind-set which had made it easier to accept that violence was a way forward. But there was little thought given to the effects of such violence or what could be gained by it. Indeed, he felt that it had only been in the last five or six years that people on both sides, especially from within those sections of our communities which had borne the brunt of the suffering, had begun to address such questions.

The second session looked at what actually happened on the streets in the late 1960s. Bernadette McAliskey, former Civil Rights activist, stated that the "problems of the '60s were not the *start*, they were the *end result* of the refusal to deal with the core problem of this state", namely the Partition of Ireland in 1920 by the British government; a problem which, she pointed out, was still not being addressed today. With Partition those who would have been among the majority in an independent Ireland now found themselves a minority in the new state of Northern Ireland, the leaders of which sought to ensure that nationalists never came to power. The mechanisms by which the latter had sought to do this finally broke down in the 1960s.

Boyd Black, giving a Unionist/Loyalist perspective, took issue with McAliskey's assertion that Partition was the root cause of the problem. The problem, as he saw it, was that two communities with divergent aspirations *already existed* in 1920, and Partition was not so much a *political* reality imposed *by* Britain, but a *social* reality imposed *upon* Britain. One set of aspirations could only have been granted by coercing the other. "Now either you say that the British government should have coerced one grouping, or that the British didn't have much alternative and took the line of least resistance." He had less sympathy for the British government for imposing a separate parliament on Northern Ireland, for this effectively excluded the people there from mainstream United Kingdom political parties and processes. Furthermore, it left power in Northern Ireland in the hands of Protestants who felt threatened and reacted accordingly, thereby increasing minority alienation. Nevertheless, this alienation was slowly decreasing by the 1950s and even the early Civil Rights movement could be viewed as an attempt to move forward through established institutions. However, the state still felt threatened and those who wished to misuse the Civil Rights movement to destroy the system were able to get the local Northern Ireland government to overreact.

In the third segment the rise of paramilitarism was charted, with Andy Tyrie, former chairman of the largest Loyalist paramilitary organisation, the Ulster Defence Association, and Tommy Gorman, IRA ex-prisoner (and escapee from the *Maidstone* prison ship), detailing their experiences of the escalating violence, and stressing that their involvement was motivated by a desire to protect their respective communities and identities. The significance of the exchange was indicated when Tyrie admitted that it was the first time he had shared a platform with a member of the IRA, and that while he felt uncomfortable about this he accepted that such encounters were inevitable.

To complement the analytical workshops, the programme included individual placements, cultural activities, field trips and a wide range of lectures – the purpose of which was to provide the visitors with a deeper insight into different facets of life in Northern Ireland. They met with individuals involved in community work, local government and Social Services provision.

They also travelled to Londonderry to hear from two practitioners in community action: Paddy Doherty and Glen Barr. Doherty, Director of Inner City Trust, sought to demonstrate that government-supported, direct self-help action aimed at social, economic, political and cultural advancement was compatible with his Irish Republicanism. Glen Barr, a leader of the Ulster Workers' Strike which brought down the 1974 power-sharing Executive, and now Director of the Maydown Ebrington Centre, a community employment project, pursued a similar role within Derry's Protestant community, although the two men often worked closely on mutually beneficial projects. Of particular interest was the two men's attempt to halt the growing segregation which had occurred on both sides of the River Foyle – a poignant reminder to the visitors whose communities were divided by the River Dniester.

One further talk which impressed the visitors was that given by Derick Wilson at the Corrymeela Centre, when he spoke on deep-rooted violent conflict, particularly with regard to Frank Wright's notion of 'ethnic frontiers':

> An 'ethnic frontier' can take different forms; in Northern Ireland it is characterised by historical circumstances whereby people of one tradition were placed in the midst of people of another tradition who had been there before them. The need to secure one's own identity meant it was always much easier to make links *within* traditions and harder to make them *across* traditions. It also led to the need to protect one's own group by discriminating against the other. But 'ethnic frontiers' – the interface lines between different groups – were often characterised by fear, and came under attack when that fear grew. Somehow we have to reach beyond this and deal with these fears and emotions. To do so we not only need a political process, we also need a process of meeting each other in small groups. This is important, for people will not trust the political process unless they also experience that same trust at first hand, and likewise I don't think the politicians will sign up to any deal unless they feel the people want it.

The Moldovan and Transdniestrian delegations found the study visit extremely valuable, one delegate saying: "After what we have learned about Northern

Ireland I think *our* reconstruction will take less time." What they had heard had also confirmed their own views on the counterproductive nature of violence.

> War will not solve our problem. Even though I am a military man (in government) I am opposed to it. If either side makes arguments in favour of their right to use force for its own position, we simply retain the grounds for future conflict.

> I am even more convinced that it is only without violence and by means of negotiations with due respect and understanding to the 'other side', even by way of very prolonged negotiations, that this is the way to a resolution of the conflict. Both parties have to accept a compromise, in the interest of the whole population.

However, the Northern Irish experience had also taught them that *prolonged* negotiations still needed to be seen to be producing results.

> I think we got a very good lesson that a very long process of negotiations where compromises are not reached, through the fault of one party or another, will bring about very bad results. We also realised how deep-rooted a conflict can become if problems are neglected. It goes from generation to generation and becomes even more deep-rooted.

> Andy [Tyrie] talked about 'half-truths' being told by both sides, and what I think is important is that here on both sides of this table – Moldovan and Transdniestrian – we are trying to create the truths for *both* sides. No-one is the bearer of 'truth' in the final instance. If we define the 'truth' as the rights belonging to a *single individual*, then we will be better able to understand the rights of communities. If we can find ways of satisfying the rights of individuals then we should also be able to satisfy the rights of groups.

Northern Irish adversaries also felt that the exchange had been very positive, even 'illuminating' in providing them with the opportunity to collectively engage in an assisted, non-threatening self-analysis. Judging by the heated exchanges which frequently punctuated the presentations of the Northern Irish speakers, it was quite evident to the visitors that the 'Irish problem' was still very much alive and close to the surface of people's emotions. At the same time it was also obvious to some of the Northern Irish participants just how little the differing interpretations of their conflict had changed over the intervening 27 years. Unionist fears of the 'internal enemy' and Republican condemnations of the 'unjust settlement' still remained largely undiluted at the core of current analyses. Some of the speakers gave no indication that, in retrospect, they now felt their positions and tactics to have been self-defeating. Indeed, little self-questioning seemed to have taken place. It was left to one of the Northern Irish observers, Bill Rutherford, a retired surgeon, to pose a fundamental question to all of the participants:

> I worked in the hospital where the majority of people wounded during

those 25 years were brought and I had to tell the relatives of people who had died that their husband or son or father or whoever was now dead. And because of this I felt the pain of what was going on here, and I think when you get close to the pain then you only have one question: 'Why?'

Camplisson, in his summing-up, made the following comments:

Sometimes it is not the things we do or say that are the most difficult things to deal with, but the things which are *not* said and the things which are not properly understood. We need to have clear understanding of our own positions: what it is we are seeking, how we are going to achieve it, whether or not the strategy we are employing is actually taking us towards our objectives – for very often the lack of clarity on all these things leads us to make decisions which can take us towards violence. And through a deeper understanding we learn that if we seek to satisfy our own needs, we must take cognisance of our adversaries' needs in a sympathetic way. Indeed, we must begin to know our enemy as well as we know ourselves. What does *he* want? Why? What do *we* want? Why? What are his perceptions of us? How do we perceive him?

To be able to reach this point usually necessitates 'third-party' assistance and there are two distinct ways such assistance can be introduced. 'Facilitators' like ourselves can help you move towards conflict resolution, while 'mediators' like the OSCE and others can assist you in constructing the necessary political framework. The two processes are separate but with care can be made complementary.

The inter-governmental delegation had been accompanied on its visit by three members of the JCDC. This linkage was deliberate on the part of MICOM, for it was considered important to demonstrate that the community-based strand of the process was complementary to the strand which engaged the political leaderships. Indeed, Camplisson specifically drew the attention of the inter-governmental delegates to the non-governmental part of the process, expressing the hope that as the process deepened the two strands would engage in more exchanges and learn from each other's experiences. That such a two-pronged approach was important was evident from the reactions of the governmental representatives to the community projects they had visited.

Some of the most important things we saw here were the initiatives that are going from the [grassroots]. They are aimed at overcoming contradictions and maintaining an atmosphere of trust. I think that Northern Ireland has accumulated a vast experience in this sphere and we have to learn from it.

The development of a positive linkage between the two strands was especially important given the mistrust which had been voiced by elements within the political leadership in Moldova who felt that they were being challenged by this new leadership emerging within the community development process in the villages, towns and cities. The deeply-ingrained, top-down approach to leadership, which had been the hallmark of the totalitarianism of the Soviet Union, was now seemingly threatened by these new leaders emerging through voluntary action at the grassroots, people who were not coming up 'through the Party' and often had quite different ideas as to what form of civil society[†] should be constructed. Camplisson had foreseen this development:

> It is our task to help them see that, if they genuinely accept the necessity for change – which they claim they do – then new types of leadership will inevitably evolve, and that they should see this as complementary to what they themselves were doing, rather than antagonistic. Certainly it is a dilemma for them. These are people who have been trained all their lives to work through a style of leadership which made them view leaders emerging at the grassroots as people who should be controlled. But it is our job to see that these new leaders are *not* brought under control, for those who are organising from below are driven by the everyday needs of ordinary people, needs to which the establishment has failed to respond, and they are seeking to address those needs in new ways, where possible in collaboration with central authority.

This perception of feeling threatened had come to a head when the JCDC had sought to hold a conference in Bender, only to have the political leaders in the town refuse to give the necessary permission, an indication of their suspicion that such a conference posed a direct challenge to the status quo from those engaged in community development efforts. Not that such a fear existed solely within a totalitarian system, as Camplisson knew only too well, for similar fears had been voiced by politicians in Northern Ireland as community action grew in strength within working-class areas of Belfast.

> There is an element of truth in their fear, for *proper* community development *is* about continuous change. It starts from the interface where the problem is most acutely felt, then moves outwards, forcing responses from, and changes within, the wider social and political system. Governments try to ensure that community development is implemented in quite the opposite way. 'Community development' agencies look at communities and say: "Yes, that community is having problems, we'll give it a dose of 'community development': we'll put in a development officer; who will devise a programme, we will pay the bill, and that should deal with the problem." Such an approach presupposes that it is the community itself which is the problem, but I would contend that rather than *being* the problem, the community in question is merely displaying *symptoms* of a problem which is located within the system as a whole. To eradicate the community's 'problem', then, *may* require fundamental system change. It is not the community development worker's role to promote, direct or frustrate such change, however, but merely to facilitate it.

---

† The term 'civil society' is often used to suggest 'ordinary community life' as distinguished from governmental and executive functions. In this book, however, the term is used in its broader sense, as being everything which is "of or in accordance with organised [civilised] society and government", embracing the rights of every citizen, and every function, within a society.

Bringing the two strands of the Moldovan process together and letting them see the positive role which grassroots community work played in Northern Ireland had its effect: when the Moldovans returned home members of the JCDC met with Fiodor Dobrov, the Chairman of the Soviet of Deputies of Bender, and it was agreed in principle to organise a joint conference, subject to an agreed theme. This was a significant gesture, especially as Bender was under two antagonistic jurisdictions and had suffered much as a consequence of the inter-communal divisions.

The day after the Moldovan/Transdniestrian party returned to Moldova a (prearranged) summit meeting took place between the two presidents. The governmental Expert Groups with responsibility for preparing the summit agenda had felt that the visit to Northern Ireland would not only provide them with the space to finalise this agenda, but the very nature of their programme in Northern Ireland might itself be conducive to a positive exchange.

During their stay in Northern Ireland, therefore, a special day had been set aside for the Expert Groups to prepare the final documentation for the coming summit. The two groups felt it was indeed a very productive day, and during the actual summit both delegations praised the Northern Ireland study visit and stressed the importance of the conflict resolution process of which the visit was a part. Branimir Radev, the Acting Head of the OSCE peace mission to Moldova, later wrote to Camplisson to convey his satisfaction with both the study visit and its outcome.

Members of the governmental Expert Groups, the JCDC and MICOM
at the Ulster People's College, Belfast.

Encouraging a shared analysis: the Albena I experience

At the beginning of May 1997 the Moldovan and Transdniestrian presidents signed a Memorandum of Agreement in Moscow. This was countersigned by the presidents of the Russian Federation and Ukraine, and the OSCE. A protocol to this agreement was signed later that same month in Moldova. In appreciation of the assistance received from MICOM an extra copy of this protocol was signed especially for Camplisson, to mark the occasion of the conferring on him of an honorary doctorate by the International University of Moldova, in recognition of his contribution to conflict resolution.

The signing of the Memorandum of Agreement had seemed to signify a new urgency being injected into the search for a settlement in Moldova. However, difficulties surrounding implementation of this agreement effectively put yet another block on momentum and meetings between the two Expert Groups ceased completely in July 1997. In the face of this new impasse, both sides requested that MICOM organise a second workshop in Northern Ireland to engage the Expert Groups, which would hopefully move the negotiating and conflict resolution processes forward once again. However, after careful consideration MICOM felt that without some preparatory work for such a workshop there was a high risk of failure.

The ongoing inability to resolve the identity-related and political differences between the two sides was in its turn frustrating attempts by both governments, as well as local community organisations and various NGOs, to confront the economic, environmental and other problems facing both Moldova and Transdniestria. Hence, it was felt that the most appropriate way to rekindle movement in the negotiations would be to highlight to the Expert Group negotiators the consequences at a grassroots level of the continued failure to achieve resolution. Hence, it was decided that the 'preparatory work' would take the form of a seminar, organised by the JCDC and MICOM, in which governmental representatives, along with the international Mediators, would be invited to enter into a shared analysis of political, social and economic realities with representatives of NGOs from both Moldova and Transdniestria.

An increasing number of NGOs had emerged in Moldova and Transdniestria which were endeavouring to fill the gaps and inadequacies in state services provision and to confront the realities of a divided society and a stagnating economy. Many NGOs saw themselves as crucial in facilitating the transition of their country to democracy, and were keen to work in partnership with the state, whilst maintaining an independent role.

The proposed seminar, therefore, would benefit the NGO sector just as much as it would the Expert Groups, by bringing NGOs and the political/ executive leaderships into a shared identification of everyday problems, and hopefully initiate a constructive and ongoing dialogue.

The Moldovan economy was split between two jurisdictions each with its own economic infrastructure: two governments, two currencies, internal customs barriers, with the bridges over the River Dniester not fully repaired and a heavy dependence on Russia for fuel and spares. Unemployment was high, wages and pensions were often in arrears, and water and electricity supplies were frequently rationed. There was mounting evidence of urgent environmental and pollution problems, as well as numerous social problems stemming from the collapse of former state enterprises and health and welfare arrangements, with pensioners and the unemployed suffering the most. The situation was one of severe economic and social hardship with little prospect of amelioration, aggravated by the inability of the two governments to resolve their conflict or even to implement previously signed agreements. It was hoped that the seminar would serve to highlight this frustrating situation, as well as prepare the way for self-help remedial action within and between both jurisdictions.

Albena, on Bulgaria's Black Sea coast, was selected, largely because of low season costs, as the location for the five-day seminar, which took place in September 1997. The seminar was attended by representatives of some of the more active and significant NGOs in both Moldova and Transdniestria. They reflected a wide variety of interests: culture and education, political studies, the media, engineering, agriculture, co-operative banking, human rights, youth organisations, women's groups, village councils, veterans' unions, legal advisors, university faculties and others. They were joined by representatives of various community organisations, professional bodies and NGOs from Northern Ireland and Great Britain. Both the Moldovan and Transdniestrian governmental Expert Groups were represented and the OSCE and Ukrainian Mediators also attended.

The primary purpose of the seminar (funded by the UK Department for International Development, DfID) was to identify and analyse problems and needs surrounding violent conflict and economic system change, develop ideas and action plans for remedy, as well as prepare for the planned study visit to Northern Ireland by the Moldovan and Transdniestrian governmental Expert Groups. To achieve this purpose, the Programme consisted of panel presentations from members of relevant NGOs from Northern Ireland and Great Britain, and a mixture of plenary sessions and workshops dealing with the following:

- an overview of life in Moldova and Transdniestria, given by Moldovan and Transdniestrian speakers;
- an overview of NGOs in civil society, with a focus on Moldovan and Transdniestrian experiences;

- an identification of problems, whether personal, functional, communal, national or international, and whether relating to social, economic, cultural, political, environmental, educational or other needs;
- a sharing of perceptions around, and an analysis of, those problems which had been identified;
- the determining of needs surrounding: the economy, social welfare, the constitutional positions, conciliation, the conflict containment and resolution processes, and mechanisms and structures for improving community relations between communities and between communities and government;
- the satisfying of community needs: with perspectives from Moldovan and Transdniestrian government representatives, as well as from the Mediators;
- a focus on needs in civil society development: individual, organisational, legal, etc.;
- experiences from the West: Northern Irish and English experiences, and lessons learned relative to taking ideas forward in Moldova and Transdniestria;
- planning, plan implementation, evaluating action: who does what, where, when, how, on return to Moldova and Transdniestria?
- resourcing plans; available options, new options; what could be done to help one another, what could/should governments do, what should the international community do?
- The way ahead and seminar review, analysis and conclusions: what worked well, what did not work, what expectations had been fulfilled, what frustrations remained, what were the implications for government policy vis-a-vis NGOs?

In his opening address Camplisson had posed a series of questions: Why are we all gathered together? What is our motivation? What are our goals? What are our hopes and aspirations? Why are we sitting down with strangers, some of whom are our adversaries? What everyone present was ultimately engaged in, he said – even if the seminar might concentrate on the day-to-day, practical needs of rebuilding civil society – was a search for a way of living together without fear of one another. And it was a search which called for a contribution from everyone.

He then asked the participants to reflect for a moment on the brutal reality of violent conflict – especially as experienced by the bereaved, by the refugees, by all of them. Those gathered at Albena were attempting, he said, to confront one of the most complex and difficult problems of our time – identity-related violent conflict. He also drew the participants' attention to the broader implications of their quest. To them, it might seem to be concerned primarily with their own particular conflict, but the very methodology they were utilising, if successful, could provide valuable lessons to all those involved in community development and conflict resolution initiatives around the world.

All participants found the seminar worthwhile and its methods challenging. The organisers were encouraged by the way in which those from different levels of leadership – non-governmental, governmental, and international bodies – found common cause and worked together in a shared identification of problems and related needs, across a wide variety of issues – from social, economic, educational, cultural and ecological concerns to human and minority rights, the role of the media, the development of civil society and democratic accountability.

The governmental representatives listened to, and expressed their gratitude for, the clearly-stated views of the NGOs. The need for a *single* economic, ecological, legal and information 'space' was clearly identified by the participants. There was wide agreement on the importance of cultural exchanges and 'people's diplomacy' across the 'peaceline' and between the various ethnic groups. Most importantly, a number of action plans were drawn up for local co-operation, especially along and across the River Dniester.

One striking feature during the course of the week had been the clear evidence of a reversal in the perceptions and attitudes towards NGOs which had been held by some of the governmental participants, particularly those not previously exposed to the community development process. One of the governmental delegation remarked: "I now have a more favourable attitude to the activity of NGOs and I will try to support them," while another expressed the opinion: "I now have increased hope for the future knowing just how many dedicated, selfless people are striving for the good of their communities."

The NGO representatives were equally enthusiastic about the seminar's impact, one saying: "From now on I will strive to seek mutual understanding; I will have respect for the position of others," while another promised: "In my future work I will invite the participation of NGOs from the other side."

The positive impact of the Albena seminar was particularly evident upon the JCDC. Their planned programme of activities, which was extensive and ambitious, received a welcome boost, and the energetic discussions on problems and related needs helped to crystalise its shape and content.

MICOM's work clearly benefited from the Albena seminar, and the linkage of the complementary strands of that work – the programme in support of the JCDC and the conflict resolution process engaging the governmental Expert Groups – was considerably enhanced. In particular, MICOM's working relationship with the Mediators and the Expert Groups was significantly advanced. During the seminar the OSCE and Ukrainian representatives, together with members of the conflict resolution facilitation team and the JCDC, framed an outline agenda for the forthcoming inter-governmental study visit to Belfast. That agenda marked an important new developmental stage in MICOM's work, for it would include a one-day seminar engaging the OSCE, Russian and Ukrainian Mediators and the conflict resolution facilitation team. This would examine their respective roles dealing with the Moldovan/ Transdniestrian conflict and how these might complement each other.

Moldovan protagonists revisit Northern Ireland

The event for which the Albena seminar had been preparation, a study visit to Northern Ireland by members of the two governmental Expert Groups accompanied by the international Mediators, took place in November 1997. The positive impact of the Albena seminar was highlighted at the commencement of the visit when Evghenii Levitsky (President Kuchma of Ukraine's plenipotentiary at the mediated negotiations) read out a letter of appreciation regarding it. The letter praised the seminar's methodology for helping to convince the participants that the will existed – on both banks of the Dniester – for co-operation. It also acknowledged that some of what was discussed at Albena had since become the basis of a new draft document between the Moldova and Transdniestrian Expert Groups, adding: "...the constructive spirit of the Albena seminar had been transferred completely onto the process of negotiations."

The participants comprised a five-strong Expert Group representing the government of Moldova (a sixth member was recalled urgently), a six-strong Expert Group representing the government of Transdniestria, all three Mediators (representing the OSCE, Russian Federation and Ukraine), and a MICOM facilitation team. Observers from MICOM's core funder, C S Mott Foundation, and the funder of the Study Visit, the UK Department of International Development, were also present. The Chairperson of the JCDC acted as an observer/consultant.

As well as the exploration of needs which had been undertaken at Albena, a questionnaire had been sent to the Expert Groups and Mediators, in which they had been further asked to identify these needs. The programme was designed to meet, as far as was possible, the various needs which had been articulated. Access to the top levels of Northern Ireland political leadership was ensured by the nature of the venues selected: the Northern Ireland Forum for Political Dialogue; Parliament Buildings, Stormont; and Belfast City Hall. The reality of the Northern Ireland conflict at grassroots level was made evident by visits to community projects straddling the 'peaceline' in Belfast. Expert lecturers provided information on matters such as UK Government legislation in Northern Ireland, cross-border initiatives and currency. Civic receptions were held to honour the visitors and help raise awareness in Northern Ireland of the existence and nature of the 'peace process' in Moldova/Transdniestria. A challenging series of discussions took place during which specific needs were addressed, especially those relating to blockages being experienced in both the mediated negotiations and the conflict resolution process in Moldova/Transdniestria.

Some of the programme highlights included:

Orientation tour of Belfast 'peaceline':

- Ainsworth Community Centre. Louis West, manager, described the centre's various activities aimed at addressing problems surrounding inter-communal violence along the Protestant/Unionist side of the 'peaceline'.
- Megabytes Café, Andersonstown Road. Jim McCorry, Director, spoke of his global perspective and his work as a Socialist Republican on the Catholic side of the 'peaceline', as well as his cross-community work. This had brought him into a long-standing relationship with the JCDC.
- Farset Youth and Community Development Project. A talk was given by Billy Hutchinson, Director of Springfield Inter-Community Development Project; Tommy Gorman, his Deputy; and Father Gerry Reynolds. Hutchinson and Gorman spoke of their respective experiences since the early 70s, which included those prior to and since their imprisonment (seventeen and thirteen years respectively). Father Reynolds spoke about his attempts to build bridges between the two main Christian traditions.

Northern Ireland Forum for Political Dialogue

After a welcome address by its Chairman, John Gorman, the Expert Groups and Mediators heard a panel presentation by members of the Forum's Political Affairs Committee. They were given a comprehensive and broadly-based Unionist analysis – Nationalists having boycotted the Forum – of the political situation in Northern Ireland.

Later, at a special meeting of the Forum, a panel presentation was made to the Northern Ireland political representatives by Anatol Taran (leader of Moldova's Expert Group), Valerii Litskai (leader of Transdniestria's Expert Group), John Evans (Head of Mission, OSCE), Ambassador Yuri Karlov (Russian Federation) and Evghenii Levitsky (Ukraine). Part of the session appeared on local television.

Also at the Forum the visitors heard two presentations. Firstly, from Linda Devlin, Northern Ireland Office, on how the two jurisdictions of Northern Ireland and the Republic of Ireland related to each other across a wide range of issues and concerns. Secondly, from Paddy Hart, International Fund for Ireland, and Tony Kennedy, Co-operation North, as to how major funding was harnessed for the purpose of bringing communities in Northern Ireland and the Republic of Ireland into a closer relationship with one another.

Belfast City Hall

At Belfast City Hall the Expert Groups were given a talk by Brian Kennedy of the Bank of Ireland on the relationship between British sterling and the Irish punt and the complexities and anomalies it gave rise to. This proved of great interest to the Moldovan and Transdniestrian delegations, for whom currency problems loomed large.

The Expert Groups also met with representatives of Sinn Féin, who gave their own equally forthright analysis of politics in Northern Ireland.

Finally, there was a civic reception hosted by the Deputy Lord Mayor, Jim Rodgers. Present were elected representatives, Unionist and Nationalist, and local community activists from projects which had supported MICOM's work.

Parliament Buildings, Stormont
Tony Canavan, Head of Section, Community Relations Unit, explained to the visitors how his unit was attempting to address the problems of a divided society by providing funding for numerous cross-community projects initiated by locally-based NGOs. Robert Crawford, Northern Ireland Office, explained to the visitors how the United Kingdom government, through its legislation, had sought to deal with the complexities of the Northern Ireland situation.

One of the main gains for the visitors was the very fact of having been given space to take a step back from their own conflict – and the stalled negotiations – and look at them from a different perspective. They also gained a deeper understanding of the Northern Ireland conflict. The continued existence of the 'peaceline' after 28 years of inter-communal conflict served not only to demonstrate to the visitors the cost of 'conflict management' but to convince them that violence did not solve problems, but merely created more. The visitors obviously learned much, their comments revealing that they had fully understood the problems still besetting the Northern Ireland 'peace process': "The Stormont Talks are being boycotted by some Unionist parties; the Forum by Nationalist parties. You only seem to have *half* a 'peace process'?"

The plethora of community groups and NGOs working at the grassroots in Northern Ireland – endeavouring to build trust between the two communities, and tackling social, cultural and humanitarian issues – was impressive, and one of the visitors expressed the opinion that such a development should be encouraged in Moldova and Transdniestria. Another commented: "Basically, our dialogue is developed on the political level. Here, in Northern Ireland, the relationships between communities are also paid attention to. I think in our conflict we should now engage people, ordinary people, as much as we can."

Yuri Ataman's description of the work undertaken by the JCDC – with limited funding and no immediate prospect of any long-term resources – was both illuminating and encouraging to facilitators and visitors alike, and revealed just what could be achieved 'on the ground'. Among numerous projects which the JCDC were assisting a number stood out as particularly noteworthy. In one, they were working with mayors from 18 villages (nine from each side of the River Dniester) to implement a programme in which they would clean up their respective stretches of the river and transform it into a nature reserve. In another, eight villages (again, four from one side of the Dniester and four from the other) were organising Christmas festivities for 400 children, during which the children would perform a concert in Transdniestria, then cross a bridge over the Dniester to perform the same concert in Moldova. Mayors from towns which had so far been suspicious and sceptical about such 'cross-community' work, had been invited along as observers.

For most of their stay the visitors had been provided, courtesy of the Northern Ireland Forum, with a specially-prepared room in the Forum building. There the two Expert Groups, the international Mediators and the MICOM facilitation team engaged in a series of explorations of the numerous problems felt to be impeding resolution of the Moldovan/Transdniestrian conflict.

Undoubtedly, one of the most important sessions which took place during the study visit was when the international Mediators and the MICOM facilitation team spent an entire day exploring the relationship between their two separate processes and how they could be made to work in a more complementary manner. It was noted that it had taken five years of confidence-building between the facilitators of both processes before their coming together like this at a seminar could be put in place. Mark Hoffman, LSE, believed that this was the first time that a needs-based conflict resolution process and a power-based mediation process had sought to achieve such a complementarity.

A striking measure of the study visit's success was provided shortly afterwards, when, following the visitors' return to Moldova, it was announced on Moldovan television that regular meetings of the Expert Groups, which had ceased in July, would resume from 4 December.

One strong impression left by the study visit was that the up to now elusive element in MICOM's conflict resolution process involving the governmental Expert Groups – assisted analysis, commencing with a 'mapping out of the conflict' – seemed almost ready to begin. But could the will to engage productively within the conflict resolution process, which was being demonstrated among local authority leaders and NGOs in Moldova and Transdniestria, be replicated within the central authority leadership?

The two observers, Robert Walker from the UK Department of International Development (DfID) and Jeanette Mansour, representing C S Mott Foundation, had also felt it was a worthwhile event. Indeed, rather than limiting her role to that of observer, Mansour had become an enthusiastic participant during the regular reviews conducted by the MICOM facilitation team.

The Joint Committee for Democratisation and Conciliation

The emergence of MICOM's local partner, the JCDC, was one of the most significant products of the Moldovan initiative. Drawing its membership equally from Moldova and Transdniestria, there was no equivalent organisation on either side. Accepted on all sides as an 'indigenous third party', its efforts to initiate and facilitate self-help social action programmes within and between Moldova and Transdniestria had gained the admiration and respect of all those closely associated with MICOM in Northern Ireland.

This had been especially so among those working at community level, for they knew only too well the many setbacks and problems which any indigenous organisation with a 'cross-community' membership and purpose had to confront. They knew too that not only would the JCDC have to contend with institutional obstructionism and grassroots suspicion, but that each member would undoubtedly have undertaken a difficult personal journey of their own.

The outbreak of violence in Moldova had been a traumatic experience for many people there. As Irina Colina, then deputy head of the Department for Health and Social Protection, and a co-founder of the JCDC, recalled:

> Before the fighting we knew that problems existed; we had discussed the current situation and its causes at home, and expressed our different opinions as to how it might develop. But for us it was unreal to think that there could be a war, that people who lived together could end up fighting each other. Even when the first shots were fired [in December 1991] I felt that surely this would make everyone think hard and that the existing problems would then be solved.

Evghenii Berdnikov, another JCDC member, experienced a similar bewilderment, particularly when so many different nationalities had previously lived side by side quite peacefully:

> I could not imagine that people who had lived together for so many years, who had created so many 'mixed' families, would divide on national principle, that events could reach a violent military conflict. But our world proved to be fragile and ordinary people suddenly found themselves completely unprotected against violence. During the conflict large numbers within the population were seized by a national psychosis. No-one wanted to listen to or hear the other side. Everyone was considering himself as the only one who was right, and was blaming everything on the other side, and was ready to go to fight against those who only yesterday had been his fellow-countrymen. We became enemies.

For many like Berdnikov the conflict was not only a communal but a personal tragedy.

> The Transdniestria conflict destroyed all my life plans, raised fears for the future and for my children. Even among my friends were people who were not able to understand what was happening and to explain it correctly. Because of this many broke off their friendship. I lost my job, took ill, and ended up in hospital with heart problems. My children found they had to behave carefully among people of other nationalities. All around was mistrust, insincerity in people's relations. My wife and I had been born in Russia and when we graduated from university we had been sent to work in Moldova – sometimes we have often thought of leaving Moldova and going back to live in Russia.

For some, the upsurge of violence precipitated their own direct involvement in the conflict, as JCDC member Valentin Romanchiuk admitted:

> The conflict touched many families directly. I myself participated in military actions. I was motivated to do that because a missile was fired into the courtyard of my home. My son was there but luckily he was not hurt. I saw innocent people being killed and I was filled with incomprehension: why are people shooting and killing, why would someone come to my house with guns? Because of the conflict I have lost some of my friends and even some relatives.

For Gheorghe and Raisa Mirzenco – who became, respectively, a member and an associate of the JCDC – the violence engulfed their own family members:

> The conflict proved to be a real tragedy for our country, as well as for us personally. Two brothers were direct participants of the war. One of them was seriously wounded and will remain forever an invalid of the war. One cousin who also participated came home without a hand and a leg – and he's a simple peasant, with three children to look after.

Some of those caught up in the conflict, whether as combatants or non-combatants, endeavoured to find answers as to its cause.

> At the beginning of the conflict I realised that such conflicts are not generated by ordinary people. Very few political leaders are truly genuine carriers of their national ideals, they are not people who honestly wish happiness and prosperity for everyone. They pursue their own interests – dreaming about being a president or a prime minister or such things – and they artificially create problems and set people to fighting one another.

Some had not only wanted to find answers, but solutions.

> I got involved in the conciliation movement to explain to myself why this had happened and to prevent something similar happening in the future.

The JCDC was initiated by the small group of people who organised the Nitra conferences alongside MICOM, people such as Irina Colina, Yuri Ataman and Mihai Voloh. The first Nitra conference threw up many difficulties, but it was an important learning experience for the organisers, as Colina recalled:

> I always believed that in any conflict there are two (or more) sides who have different interests. Therefore it is always necessary to hear the views of all sides, and only then can there be an agreement and decisions can be taken. In 1992 I was not sure who was right and who wasn't. I heard opinions from both sides with which I was not able to agree, but for me it was evident that people on both sides suffered, and that they wanted peace and prosperity. Participating in discussions at the conference I came to the thought that something should be done that will help people to realise that there is another side, and that will help them to have objective information.

When the JCDC declared its aim of bringing all sides to the conflict together it seemed they were embarking upon an impossible task, but nevertheless for some it offered the only hope, as Berdnikov reflected:

> I had a desire to stop the violence, the growing military conflict, a desire to restore the trust between people who were now confronting each other – these were the main motivations for my participation in an initiative aimed at the creation of a better society. When the proposal for such an activity came from Irina Colina I accepted straight away. I was not sure that my participation in the work of the Joint Committee would produce any real results. After the bloody events in Bender, to try and unite people, or restore confidence, presented us with a very daunting challenge. But we all understood that this required time and the efforts of many people involved in the conflict.

The JCDC, in its early days, was not without its own problems.

> Our Committee could only achieve positive results if we could reach a certain degree of agreement among our own members. This was not always the case, and that was why there had sometimes been doubt that we could resolve anything. My own hesitation increased when one of our colleagues wrote a very negative article in the newspapers about our initiative. It shocked the other members and he was expelled.

Even the first events organised by the JCDC members would only have added to such doubt.

> At the beginning, especially at the first Nitra conferences, there was constraint, mistrust and tension between the participants. Some times the sides openly blamed each other for the conflict. The unwillingness of one side to understand the needs of the other often created anger and the desire to interrupt any dialogue. But gradually the 'communication ice' began to thaw; we started to listen to and understand each other.

The JCDC persevered in its efforts and eventually began to obtain results.

> Then the Committee members organised a few cross-community events

that had a positive impact; especially effective was the third Nitra conference. That conference was attended by many people of different ages, sex, background and nationality, representing the conflicting sides. The mutual understanding that was reached between all these people was very important after the conference. People made new friends, exchanged addresses, agreed on new meetings and parted mutually satisfied.

The impact of MICOM upon the JCDC in those early days was crucial to its growing strength and self-confidence, as Evghenii Berdnikov acknowledged:

From the very beginning I could see in MICOM and its leader Djo Camplisson a lot of practical and theoretical expertise in the realm of resolution of local conflicts. Working with MICOM were people who had been on both sides of the barricades in Northern Ireland and they could share with us their experiences. We believed in Djo and his colleagues. It was the methodology recommended by MICOM that allowed us to build our work correctly with the conflicting communities. And it is important to mention also the huge amount of work that was done by MICOM in helping us to search out funding, and involving in our work the Expert Groups and the official Mediators. I consider that the work of Djo and MICOM deserves much gratitude from this society.

Valentin Romanchiuk concurred with this sentiment:

I was surprised by the professionalism of the members of MICOM, by their skills and their desire to conciliate people, to find common ground, to share with us their experiences and to teach us to resolve everything by peaceful means, to convince everyone that wars, conflicts and terrorism should not come with us into the 21st Century. Because of my experience with JCDC and MICOM I have started to listen more carefully to the opinion of other people; I have revised my dogmas on some issues and gradually I've started to resolve my problems – analysing them, looking for compromises, common points. I try to avoid 'burning issues' if I see that the time is not right for their resolution.

And, as Yuri Ataman, current chairman of the JCDC and one of its two representatives on the MICOM executive, confirmed:

There are limits to what indigenous organisations can do, and I think it is necessary to have an outside body coming in. From inside the country you cannot see everything; the people who are suffering the conflict often do not have a clear understanding of that conflict, and few have a balanced and objective judgement of what happened and what should be done. There is a need for a period of stillness when people can sit down and think about such things. But even when people come to believe that their conflict can be solved by peaceful means, many of them still don't have any idea how to go about it. That is why groups like MICOM can help, especially when they have direct experience of conflict in other countries. Often the problem is how to start things moving, for even

45

when people are not actually fighting they might still feel unable to talk to each other.

The impact of the JCDC was felt at both a personal and at a societal level, as Berdnikov explained:

I have come to realise that in Transdniestria and Moldova there are many people who sincerely wish to have a resolution of the Transdniestrian conflict. Through working with the Committee and with MICOM the most important conclusion I made was that it is possible for an NGO to achieve important results in the search for resolution of our conflict. Our work has drawn the attention of our communities and of the political and state leaders. Since 1992 we have created many positive results and involved hundreds of new people in the peace process. We have promoted very constructive initiatives aimed at the resolution of the conflict and community development, which have contributed to the restoration of confidence among our people. The Albena conference showed the high organisational level reached by the joint work of JCDC and MICOM. It also showed that this society needs our work and there is still a lot of that work ahead of us.

Valentin Romanchiuk would agree fully with that assessment:

In the beginning I was not sure that the problems could be solved and I am not sure even now that they will be, but what the Committee does is move us with small steps towards resolution. We can see results and this is positive. There was a time when the work of the Committee was in a deadlock and they were even doubts if it would be able to exist, but Yuri, Irina and Djo and the other members managed to wave off my doubts. I was most content at Albena when I saw the real results of JCDC and MICOM's work. Much of the former animosity had disappeared, and even when someone was defending his views it was done in a manner that tried to avoid offence against the other side. I also feel content because our Committee is known at different official levels and among NGOs and they all speak highly about it.

Gheorghe Mirzenco, however, would add a note of caution:

Belonging to JCDC has had an influence on my personal behaviour. I have become more tolerant towards the 'opposite side', I try to understand deeper the genesis of the conflict and the promoters of the conflict. I think there are two types of people: ordinary people who were involved in the conflict involuntarily, and politicians who were largely responsible for it. Such a division has been confirmed through our activities. When I met some of the politicians at first I felt that on the one hand they condemned the conflict but on the other they were content with such a situation because it created opportunities for them to stay on top of a power pyramid. Despite this, I decided to continue my contacts with them, hoping to be able to influence them. However, even now it concerns me that some politicians are actually profiting from the attention given to them by foreigners – MICOM, OSCE, etc. – and if they solve the conflict they will no longer be the centre of attention.

Within the JCDC, hopes for the future existed side by side with uncertainties, a reality which Valentin Romanchiuk voiced:

My initial hopes to resolve the problems in a short time have unfortunately not been realised. This will be a very long task. Even if at the grassroots there are positive results, in my opinion the higher levels have become more and more estranged. The one positive thing is that both sides understand that through violence these problems cannot be solved – that is a path to nowhere. I still have hope for the future that the sides shall put away any ambitions, shall reach an agreement and start to work on concrete economic and social protection issues. The economic situation for both sides becomes worse each day and that concerns me. It might lead to protests and public disobedience by large masses of the population, and in such conditions some leaders might possibly be ready to point to the 'enemy', claiming that it is the other side which is guilty for all our misfortunes. I hope JCDC and MICOM shall take this into consideration and strengthen their work to prevent my concerns from becoming a reality.

As Yuri Ataman explained, there was an inherent danger if efforts to achieve resolution became prolonged:

Ordinary people are not really applying enough pressure on their governments, and except for those living in or near the security zone, many people don't want to think about it too much. There was a poll conducted recently asking people what they saw as the most acute problems and very few named the Transdniestrian situation as one of them. Also, because most people feel the political leaderships don't want to resolve it, they too become apathetic.

Even though the conflict only really broke out in 1992 we have a new generation who are becoming adults under the present circumstances, and there has been little work done with them to overcome the post-conflict syndrome. There are students today in Transdniestria who cannot imagine Transdniestria having a different status to what it has now, they see it as indefinite. We see our work as trying to keep communities in touch with each others' needs, and not to allow any separation to become even deeper. If today's leaders cannot solve this conflict because of their present mentality, then it will be left to the next generation, but how the next generation thinks will depend on how they are educated *now* about the conflict. If they are educated as 'patriots' on each side then the problems will just get deeper. However, I think that the conflict resolution process has helped some of our leaders to see, for the first time, that a political settlement alone will not solve our problems and that there will be a lot of work needed after such an agreement.

Association of Mayors 'study visit'

As part of their community development programme, MICOM and the JCDC were helping to address the complex problems confronting village councils in the transition from communism and the command economy to a mixed economy and democratic structures and institutions. Many village councils were represented by the Association of Mayors (AOM), which had 120 members drawn from all parts of Moldova. To assist the JCDC and the AOM strengthen their relationship a special 'study visit' to Northern Ireland was arranged for representatives of the AOM in July 1998.

The study visit comprised two basic elements through which it sought to achieve its purpose: (1) a series of study settings, in which the visitors were given slide shows and talks at a wide variety of community development enterprise locations; (2) formal discussion/analysis in appropriate environments.

The Study Settings
A full day was spent at Belfast City Hall, where Rev. Roy Magee's reflections on the conflict between the two traditions generated much interest.

A visit to Draperstown Rural College proved highly relevant to the Moldovans. They were given important insights into why this deprived area found it necessary to have its own study facilities, which provided local people with the necessary skills to create jobs within their community.

A visit to County Donegal, just across the border in the Republic of Ireland, included the Ballyconnell Community Development Project in Falcarragh. The visitors heard about the struggle by local people to rejuvenate an area which had been steadily losing population and experiencing social and economic blight. The Project had helped turn this situation around.

There was a talk on the EU Special Support Programme for Peace and Reconciliation through which the Ballyconnell Project had been able to gain assistance. The Project's Director, Paul Skinnader, detailed how an area suffering from high levels of unemployment, few resources, poor soil and with little going for it except beautiful scenery, could be rejuvenated. The Manager, Michael Murray, offered further insights into just what a local community could achieve once it began to receive even limited funding.

Also in Donegal, the Dunlewy Project proved to be of great interest. This was a community-based tourism development project, in which the local people, conscious of the richness of their culture, were not trying to 'sell' it, but to 'share' it. Seamus Gallagher, the Project Manager, talked about its strong emphasis on community development as well as environmental concerns.

Back in Northern Ireland, at a civic lunch in Carrickfergus Fraser Agnew spoke about the continuing work between Northern Ireland and Moldova and of its impact on conflict resolution work in Northern Ireland itself. Janet Crampsey, mayor of Carrickfergus, welcomed the visitors, and the Economic Development Officer for the borough, Stella McArdle, gave a presentation on the council's economic programme and the self-help initiatives being supported by the council.

The formal sessions

As well as a number of feedback opportunities to evaluate the impact of the study settings, a number of formal sessions – facilitated by Yuri Ataman, Ian Bell, Joe Camplisson, Jonathan Cohen[†], Mark Hoffman, Lord Hylton, new MICOM member Susan Allen Nan[††], and Anne Radford[†††]– were given over to in-depth analysis and discussion.

- Weaknesses within the community development and conflict resolution processes were examined, as well as how they could be addressed.

- The general and specific needs of the participants surrounding their aspirations, concerns, problems, and developmental requirements – functional and personal – were also addressed.

- A central focus was placed on the inculcation of necessary skills within the participants, in whatever areas they felt these skills to be required – personal, professional, social, economic, political, cultural or organisational.

- An assessment was made of deteriorating economic circumstances and recent regressive political developments in Moldova and Transdniestria, and how these were frustrating attempts at conflict resolution and civil society development.

The Study Visit proved highly successful, with its stated objectives being largely met. Some unexpected movement occurred with regard to organisational development. During the final evaluation session it emerged that the AOM, prior to arrival in Northern Ireland, had greatly misunderstood the role of the JCDC and had harboured unspoken suspicions. The supportive and constructive environment generated during the study visit, however, had allowed these to be articulated, and after a period of clarification the misgivings were allayed and a stronger relationship established between the two organisations.

The Moldovan participants were also reinforced in the view that for economic development to be successful a collaborative approach was essential, especially within the security zone, and that, ultimately, the conflict had to be dealt with.

[†]   Jonathan Cohen was Director of Conciliation Resources, London.

[††]   Susan Allen Nan, subsequently a successful doctoral candidate at George Mason University (GMU), became a member of staff, Carter Centre, Georgia, USA. In 1999 she was to publish her GMU dissertation *Complementarity and Coordination of Conflict Resolution Efforts in the Conflicts over Abkhazia, South Ossetia, and Transdniestria.*

[†††] Anne Radford was a mediator in the voluntary sector who had worked with a number of international charities, helping them deal with internal management/worker conflicts.

Return to Bulgaria: Albena II

As a follow-up to the highly successful 1997 Albena seminar, a second, week-long seminar, again funded by DfID, was held there in September 1998. Present were journalists, businessmen, parliamentarians, students, housewives, lawyers, teachers, military personnel, as well as representatives of NGOs, local and national authorities, national minorities and others. There were specialists and facilitators from Moldova/Transdniestria, Northern Ireland, Great Britain, United States, Poland, Germany and Romania. Importantly, as at Albena I, there were representatives of the Moldovan and Transdniestrian governmental Expert Groups. Also present were: General Roman Harmosa, the OSCE Deputy Head of Mission; Vladimir Ustinov, the Russian Federation deputy mediating ambassador; Evghenii Levitsky, President Kuchma's plenipotentiary Ukrainian mediator; and George Roman, Co-Chair of the Joint Control Commission (responsible for the joint peace-keeping force).

By addressing community development needs and conflict resolution in a complementary way, the general purpose of the seminar was to facilitate interaction between governmental and non-governmental sectors in Moldova and Transdniestria so as to let the former hear about the lives and conditions of ordinary people, and for both to begin to find ways of working together in the development of civil society and participative democracy. It was also hoped that the processes of mediated negotiations and conflict resolution would gain impetus and purpose from such interaction.

Complementing this general purpose were two important aims:

- To bring the JCDC and its individual members to the higher levels of competence and confidence necessary to respond meaningfully to the ever-widening variety and complex nature of their tasks. Focus was on any difficulties preventing a full collaboration with others, at all levels of leadership and across the spectrum of needs – social, economic, political, etc. – in Moldova/Transdniestria as well as, increasingly, the region.

- To effect a meaningful resumption of the regular monthly mediated negotiations between the Expert Groups – now stalled yet again – and to bring the Expert Groups and the international Mediators into more productive relationships with each other, with those at other levels of leadership within Moldova and Transdniestria – voluntary organisations, NGOs, mayors, etc. – and with the MICOM facilitation team.

Seminar design was by Barney McCaughey, who co-facilitated with Camplisson. The non-governmental representatives were engaged in small group and plenary report-back workshops; they also formed themselves into special interest groups whose purpose was to identify problems and to prepare action plans.

The Expert Groups and the international Mediators held their own workshops, within which the MICOM conflict resolution team – Mark Hoffman, Susan Allen Nan, Diana Francis and Camplisson – facilitated an exploration of the idea of a 'common state'. The workshops were also aimed at assisting preparations for a resumption of the mediated negotiations and the attempts at conflict resolution.

Significantly, NGOs and government representatives, in an unofficial capacity, came together in the plenary sessions to work on the identification, review and analysis of problems and related needs, and how these might be addressed by all levels of leadership working collaboratively within and between both jurisdictions.

An important theme running through the seminar was a focus on the personal responsibility of those in conflict and on making the link between personal needs and aspirations and global needs. A challenging aspect of the Action Plan preparation was the suggestion that 'oneself' be included as party to the problem by omission. Taking personal responsibility through action with others transformed that individual into a dynamic for change.

The workshops began with an identification of the problems which affected people living in a conflict situation. Numerous key problems and issues emerged from within the NGO and local authorities' groupings, encompassing a wide range of concerns: psychological, economic, social, ecological, cultural, political, legal; and related to minority rights, individual rights, information access, etc.

Once a general overview of such problems had been completed, a number of priorities were drawn from the initial plenary report-back session as the basis for 'special interest' workshops. These were: Political Relations and Processes; Economy/Small Businesses/Self-Help; Human Rights/Community Relations/Language; Young People's Problems; Women's Issues; Mass Media; Local Authorities. In these 'special interest' workshops, key issues were identified, as were those individuals and agencies who were involved in meeting needs, and, finally, action plans for remedy were agreed upon.

It would be impossible here to do justice to the wealth of material which resulted from the seminar. One participant referred to it as "a basket of ideas and thoughts" which "could help our politicians to move forward towards real solutions." Others asked that this 'basket of ideas' be compiled as a database. The head of the Transdniestrian Expert Group said that all of the ideas expressed should not be wasted and should be made available to the Expert Groups for possible incorporation into documents arising from the negotiation process. Exposure to the seminar discussion also impacted on the views of the leader of the Moldovan Expert Group who felt that it revealed to him that the social basis of the conflict was much narrower than he had previously thought.

In terms of on-the-ground interaction there was a real engagement and a constructive dialogue between the governmental and non-governmental participants. The Expert Groups elected to work with the general body in both the small group and plenary sessions. Questions were asked and points of clarification requested. The genuineness of the communication was reflected in its occasionally fraught nature. Feedback into plenary sessions from the special interest groups informed the Expert Groups' negotiations and vice versa.

Relationships between NGOs on either side of the Dniester
Satisfaction in meeting people with similar interests and commitment and in establishing positive relationships was evident throughout the seminar and was indicated in the discussion regarding the 'database', for, while important for politicians, it would also be a valuable tool for NGO networking. The early introduction of small-group work around areas of special interest facilitated initial in-depth sharing, and in the course of the week the groups defined and redefined themselves until, in the end, some of the groups, including members from each side of the Dniester, formed themselves into actual *action*, as opposed to simply *interest*, groups.

It was evident, especially from the discussions within the special-interest group dealing with political issues, that although there were significant political differences between people from either side of the Dniester there was nonetheless a general commitment to work towards a solution acceptable to both sides, and, where possible, to collaborate on confronting the problems they each lived with as a consequence of the conflict and the systems change which they were undergoing (and, indeed, bringing about).

Participants commented on the significantly reduced levels of hostility between themselves in comparison with previous years. They described themselves as friends. It was therefore not surprising, although it seemed to have symbolic value, that at the reconvening of the regional groups on the last day of the seminar, there had to be a reconstitution of the *previously separate* Moldovan and Transdniestrian groups into *mixed* Moldovan/Transdniestrian groups because they no longer saw value in working separately.

Interaction between NGOs and Local Government representatives
Discussion indicated that misconceptions concerning the integrity of the work of NGOs had existed in the minds of some local authorities. Constructive work was done both in discussing these concerns openly and in exposing this level of government to the nature of NGO work represented in the seminar. Significant progress was evident in the fact that there were stated intentions on the part of local authorities to find out more about the work of NGOs in their regions, and to co-operate with them where appropriate. The mayor of

Cremenchuik, for example, made close contacts with members of NGOs from Moldova as well as Transdniestria in order to work on the issue of women's unemployment.

Co-operation between Local Authorities from each bank of the Dniester
The Association of Mayors was able to report on the ongoing work between the districts Slobozia (Transdniestria) and Stefan-Voda (Moldova), in the 'Bridge of Trust' project, involving the villages on each side in local marketing and cultural exchanges. Information was provided, and support asked for, in relation to their follow-up work. The mayors of Rybnitsa and Rezina were able to formulate action plans on one of the issues they both had on their agenda – co-operation on Moldovan language provision.

Relationships between different arenas of conflict
Information about other conflicts, as well as listening to and experiencing the feelings and behaviour of people recently involved in conflict, such as the Northern Irish participants, had a significant impact on the discussions and, indeed, the atmosphere of the proceedings. The Northern Irish described the deep trauma both their communities had suffered, and yet, at the same time, they also presented an affecting image of what peace was about, for they each acknowledged personal flaws in dealing with one another and quite clearly acted in ways which showed their concern for, and support of, one another, despite strongly held political differences.

It was regrettable that two associates from Kosovo (one Serb, one Albanian) had been unable to attend due to illness. Information about different post-Soviet conflicts in the process of systems transition fed into discussions about economics and the recurring question of national minority rights. In the latter case it threw new light on the issue, defusing its immediate heat by allowing discussion in the context of someone else's conflict. It also raised the question of majority rights.

Relationship between Mediators and MICOM/JCDC
The events of Albena 1998 undoubtedly deepened the relationship between the Mediators and both MICOM and the JCDC. The Russian Mediator, in his presentation, noted that this relationship had been spoken about in the Expert Group discussions, where its importance had been acknowledged. "Much depends on you in the case of negotiations between Transdniestria and Moldova. Each time they come together and talk can provide a unique opportunity." Both the representative of Ukraine in Moldova and the Deputy Chief of the OSCE mission in Moldova gave generously of their time to present their experiences of situations of conflict in Crimea and Poland respectively. The latter closed his presentation by saying: "I hope that the results of this seminar should be fruitful, not only to ourselves, but to the leaders of the

[Expert Group] delegations. Indeed, they should be useful for every intelligent person."

Seminar outputs included:

Developments related to conflict resolution and the inter-governmental mediated negotiation process

- During the seminar, with governmental participation, there was a strengthening of the desire, already in place among ordinary people, to see movement towards the resolution of conflict.
- The making of plans and preparations for the resumption of the stalled inter-governmental negotiations was a manifestation of positive movement. (The negotiations resumed on 7 October.)
- Government representatives to the negotiations, together with representatives of the OSCE, the Russian Federation and Ukraine, developed collaborative relationships at the seminar with middle (local authority) and lower (local community) levels of leadership across a wide range of shared concerns, including the conflict. Feedback from the special interest workshops informed the Expert Groups' negotiations and vice versa.
- Shortly after the seminar the Moldovan representative on the Joint Control Commission (the body overseeing peace-keeping forces in the Security Zone) informed the JCDC that the number of Moldovan troops in the Security Zone was being reduced following discussions on the subject at Albena.

Developments relating to the NGO and community development process

- The JCDC believed that the seminar made a significant contribution to the post-violence healing process.
- Participants at all levels spoke of how they were moved psychologically and emotionally by their experiences at the seminar. There was a perceptible move away from entrenched positions, allowing for movement on the development of shared ideas and action plans.
- NGO and local government plans were to be taken forward for implementation on return to Moldova/Transdniestrian, as well as to Northern Ireland.

The Albena seminar was an important boost to the community development strategy, advancing the conflict resolution process contained within it, as well as the self-help efforts ongoing at local community level. Perhaps, however, it was the interaction between the different levels of leadership which was its most significant, and possibly unique, aspect.

Respite – the field of play

Despite highly successful events such as the two Albena seminars and the various study visits, where MICOM's interventions had been able to assist the governmental Expert Groups to overcome each impasse in their mediated negotiations, MICOM had been unable to engage them jointly in a full process of assisted analysis, aimed at examining their own and each others' positions, as well as those seemingly self-defeating strategies they were adopting to achieve their objectives. Such a process, MICOM felt, was the only realistic way to engender movement towards resolution of the conflict. While there was productive movement away from the danger of a return to war there was no evidence of a will within the Expert Groups to move away from their current positions towards conflict resolution. During Albena, however, tentative discussions had taken place regarding a forthcoming event MICOM felt might engender more impetus for such movement – and that event was a football match.

In February 1998 President Lucinschi, Moldova, and Igor Smirnov, Transdniestria, had been met in their respective capitals by Camplisson and Lord Hylton. In the course of the meetings Camplisson, in a jocular manner, had said to each leader that he was planning a 'summit workshop' in Belfast for both presidents on 18 November 1998. The fact that Moldova was to play Northern Ireland in Belfast on that day in a European Championship match, had, 'of course', no bearing on his reasoning. The idea of such a visit somehow got into a Moldovan newspaper the following day. The Head of the OSCE mission in Moldova, John Evans, USA, told MICOM that such a visit would, in his opinion, greatly assist the search for a solution to the Moldovan/Transdniestrian conflict.

A group of MICOM's associates in Belfast – Tommy Dickson, Louis West, Fraser Agnew and Alan Hewitt – persuaded Jim Boyce, president of the Irish Football Association, to extend an invitation to the match to both presidents. A further invitation went from Dr Mo Mowlam, Secretary of State for Northern Ireland. In the event, due to serious domestic and regional difficulties, necessitating the attention of both presidents, only a Moldovan emissary team was able to come, led by ambassador Ion Leshanu.

However, an unexpected benefit emerged from the changed circumstances, in that it provided an opportunity to focus on the needs of the Moldovan governmental representatives. The Northern Ireland conflict experience had shown that while it was vital to engage protagonists in a shared process, it could be important and productive to engage each protagonist separately.

As well as in-depth workshops and discussions, the programme also included its usual mixture of civic receptions, interactive cross-communal activities and social events – all now the hallmarks of any MICOM venture. The main components of the programme were:

- MICOM associates Michael Hall and Alan Hewitt gave the visitors a tour of the 'peace-lines' in North and West Belfast, highlighting the physical and environmental impact made on both communities by such stark divisions. The fact that a new section of 'peaceline' had to be built only months before their visit was a reminder that when political leaders fail to remove the underlying causes of distrust then the generational character of such barriers is assured.

- At Parliament Buildings, Stormont, the visitors heard presentations from a number of local politicians – representing the full range of political opinion in Northern Ireland – who gave their respective party positions on the current state of the peace process, and highlighted important factors which had led to the new possibilities, as well as dangers, which now existed.

- And, of course, the Northern Ireland v Moldova European Championship match (which ended in a 'win-win' outcome – 2:2), where the Moldovans were guests at a pre-match dinner at Windsor Park. Jim Boyce, for the Irish Football Association, in welcoming Ambassador Leshanu and his delegation, wished them success in their quest for resolution of the conflict in Moldova.

At Parliament Buildings, Stormont (where they had exclusive use of a room for the week), the visitors had a discussion on the Belfast Agreement (also known as the 'Good Friday Agreement') led by Jackie Johnston from the Northern Ireland Office. He explained that the Agreement was the culmination of seven years' work to build a common agenda. Near the end of the series of discussions which led to the Agreement and the subsequent Northern Ireland Assembly, various threads had to be tied together: the 'three strands' of the relationships involved (within Northern Ireland, between Northern Ireland and Republic of Ireland, and between the Republic of Ireland and Great Britain); confidence-building measures; policing; prisoners; an election process for the inclusion of smaller parties; the building of a climate of trust and open agendas; and the issue of constitutional sovereignty.

The Moldovans asked questions about numerous aspects of the process which had led to the Agreement, in particular concerning areas such as: what role the international community, especially the USA and Senator Mitchell, had played; what constitutional changes – as well as constitutional guarantees – were required to make the Agreement work; what delegation of authority to Northern Ireland was anticipated, and what was the nature of that authority; what the *mechanisms* of negotiations had been, and whether there had been any interim agreements or only the final document; whether all parties expressed their ideas freely, and whether the details of the discussions were secret or public; and what were the proposed mechanisms for building trust.

With regard to the last point it was felt that informal mechanisms were vital, not just formal guarantees. This required different levels of confidence building and communication.

No doubt had the Transdniestrians been present – an apology for their absence was received and accepted – other questions might have been raised, particularly on areas relevant to the Transdniestrians' assertion of independent statehood. However, in retrospect, some of the MICOM team felt that such questions might have put the Moldovan delegation on the defensive. It was felt useful, therefore, that they had been given the chance to explore the Belfast Agreement on their own and from their own perspective.

As this analysis of the Belfast Agreement was felt by the Moldovan party to have been invaluable, not the least because it raised pointers which they must inevitably take cognisance of in their own negotiations, Mark Hoffman, LSE, provided the following synopsis of the main points of Jackie Johnston's presentation of the Agreement:

The Belfast Agreement could be explored through four main aspects:

(a)   The Principles underlying the process
(b)   The Nature of the process
(c)   The Content of the Agreement
(d)   Its Implementation

(a)   The Principles underlying the process

1.   Inclusiveness
2.   Consensus (i.e. nothing agreed until everything agreed)
3.   Transparency
4.   Non-violent resolution of the conflict
5.   Consent

(b)   The Nature of the process

1.   All parties agreed to the agenda (this part had taken seven years).
2.   Finally getting an acceptable third party to chair the negotiations.
3.   Range of different formats utilised (bi-laterals, tri-laterals, open discussions).
4.   Changes in roles of outside parties such as Great Britain and the Republic of Ireland – e.g. no longer any vested interest in Northern Ireland. (Would this have resonances with Russia and Ukraine?)
5.   Confidence-building measures along the way, including at community level and on cross-border links.
6.   Willingness to take risks by the leaders.
7.   The role that 'framework documents' play – spelling out principles and outcomes without deciding anything.
8.   The idea of imposing a deadline.

(c) The Content of the Agreement

1. Accept whole Agreement – holistic approach – no 'cherry-picking' (i.e. implementing only favourable parts).
2. Interrelated agreement clauses – movement and consolidation on one strand dependant on same in other strands.
3. Eventually constitutional changes required all round (in the UK and in Republic of Ireland).
4. The range of political, social and economic issues it sought to address (to allay people's fears).

(d) The Implementation of the Agreement

Now facing difficulties in Northern Ireland as the process moved to translate agreed principles into practice.

Lord Hylton (whose daughter, Emily Jolliffe, had become Camplisson's assistant, providing him with much-needed administrative support) felt that as well as the new Northern Ireland Assembly, the two other major components of the Belfast Agreement – the North-South bodies in Ireland and the British-Irish Council – could be of interest to Moldova and Transdniestria. The latter component, he felt, could be a model for a new regional grouping linking Moldova, Ukraine and Romania, with possibly Bulgaria and Belarus. The ability of the residents of Northern Ireland to choose British or Irish passports was also noted by the visitors.

The main benefits of the visit were twofold: Ambassador Leshanu gave a very positive assessment of the impact the visit to Belfast had made on his party, while Yuri Ataman was able to cement further the working relationship which had been progressively developing between government and the JCDC.

Drumcree – ghost of battles past

During the July 1988 Study Visit to Northern Ireland by the Association of Mayors, what had become known as the 'Drumcree stand-off' had again reached crisis point.[†] Roadblocks erected by Loyalist protesters had forced changes to MICOM's programme, with the Moldovan and Transdniestrian visitors at one stage effectively isolated in their hotel. Two members of MICOM's facilitation team, Mark Hoffman and Susan Allen Nan, were asked by MICOM associates, Fraser Agnew and Alan Hewitt, both Orangemen, whether they felt there was anything the 'Moldovan format' could offer to a resolution of the situation at Drumcree. They responded that first they would have to determine the *nature* of the problem, and arranged to meet separately with a representative of the Garvaghy Road Residents' Coalition and a representative of the Portadown District Orange Lodge. Although time constraints prevented anything from developing from these soundings, Hoffman and Allen Nan were of the opinion that the 'Moldovan format' *could* prove useful.

In January 1999 MICOM was again asked to explore possibilities for assistance regarding Drumcree. A discussion paper was prepared by Camplisson and Hall and presented to relevant individuals. However, although some of them agreed that the process outlined in the document did offer a way forward, they felt they were not in a position to embrace it until such time as the other processes they were engaged in had been allowed to run their course.

This request was also an indication of the increasing interest which existed in Northern Ireland, especially at community level, about the 'peace process' in Moldova. Among the numerous individuals and groups (over 150 at one count) in Northern Ireland who had assisted MICOM's Moldovan exchanges, a core group of community activists had emerged who set themselves the task of assessing whether any of the lessons learned in Moldova could be usefully transferred to the Northern Ireland situation. This group, calling itself the 'Local Community Initiative', ultimately became the main conduit through which MICOM's work in Moldova simultaneously fed into the efforts going on, at all levels of leadership, within the Northern Ireland peace process.

---

† In July 1995 the Royal Ulster Constabulary (RUC) were involved in a stand-off with Portadown Orangemen after the latter were prevented from marching from Drumcree church along the 'nationalist' Garvaghy Road (formerly a 'traditional route' before demographic changes meant that the Road now went past a Catholic housing estate). A compromise agreement eventually allowed the marchers through.

In July 1996 the RUC again prohibited the Orangemen from marching, but this time there was no agreement with the residents, and a more serious stand-off resulted. Three days of Loyalist rioting across the province finally led the RUC to reverse their tactics, and they forced the marchers through against the opposition of the residents. Days of rioting then ensued in Nationalist areas.

In July 1997, when the Orangemen were again prevented from marching, they initiated a permanent protest presence which, as this book goes to press – June 2002 – is still in place.

Confidence marked

The Northern Ireland international football team was due to play the return leg of its European Championship match against Moldova on 31 March 1999. MICOM and the JCDC felt that this would be an ideal opportunity to organise a follow-up to the September 1998 Albena II seminar, with Moldova as the venue. This would engage the Expert Groups, the international Mediators, mayors, students, NGOs, members of the Joint Control Commission and others, in a week of follow-up activities. An important component would be an inter-parliamentary seminar, following the suggestion made at Albena that a useful purpose might be served by bringing parliamentarians from both Moldova and Transdniestria into a closer relationship with the conflict resolution process.

Coincidentally, two quite separate sets of circumstances were to impact upon the proposed programme. Firstly, discussions in Northern Ireland around the Belfast Agreement were experiencing major difficulties, and the Secretary of State for Northern Ireland, Mo Mowlam, scheduled a further series of discussions, which it was hoped would break the growing impasse, for the end of March. This meant that those Northern Ireland Assembly members who had agreed to engage with their Moldovan and Transdniestrian counterparts in the inter-parliamentary seminar were unable to do so.

Secondly, increasing tensions created by the crisis in Kosovo impacted negatively within Moldova and Transdniestria. The serious differences of opinion between NATO and Russia in their approach to the crisis were mirrored by differences of opinion between the Moldovan and Transdniestrian leaderships. As a consequence, Transdniestrian parliamentarians were prevented from engaging with their Moldovan counterparts in planning for a possible May seminar to replace that postponed from March.

A rescheduled seminar was eventually agreed for September, only for the political situation in Northern Ireland to intervene once more. The failure by the Northern Ireland political parties to meet the deadline for implementing the Belfast Agreement necessitated the calling of a Review by US senator George Mitchell. The review period included September and this meant that the Northern Ireland Assembly members would again be unable to leave Northern Ireland.

Given these circumstances, it was decided that instead of an inter-parliamentary seminar one would be organised which would engage the mayors, heads of local administration and NGOs from Moldova and Transdniestria, as well as members of the Joint Control Commission – and opinion in both Moldova and Transdniestria was that this could prove to be a viable and potentially more effective alternative. Given the lingering tensions engendered by the crisis in Kosovo, with some Serbian refugees displaced to Transdniestria, it was decided that the venue for this replacement seminar would again be neutral Albena.

Despite the original March seminar having been abandoned, a MICOM team had nevertheless visited Moldova for the 31 March football fixture, and to make preparations for the forthcoming September seminar. Their flight from Budapest to Chisinau was delayed because of overhead NATO operations related to the Kosovo crisis, and when they arrived in Moldova they found the political climate tense and uncertain. An indication of the state of affairs was revealed when a fact-finding visit to Moldova by two members of the UK Foreign and Commonwealth Office, coincidentally taking place at the same time as the football match, was advised by John Evans, Head of the OSCE Mission to Moldova, not to go to Transdniestria.

Despite these difficulties, the previous relationships and trust established by MICOM and the JCDC enabled them to work through this period of uncertainty and instability, keeping options open, maintaining dialogue and networks.

The hopes which had been placed in the activities planned around the football match, for example, were partly realised. These activities had aimed to help both presidents achieve in Moldova that which had eluded them in Belfast in November 1998 – the first public demonstration, since the war, of conviviality and of a return to normal politics and diplomacy. Such a symbolic act, it had been hoped, would begin to replace despondency and despair, bringing optimism to their people.

Although there was no coming together of the two presidents at the match, senior political representatives from both Moldova and Transdniestria did attend the match as guests of MICOM, supporting their national football team 'as one'. The general public were encouraged by Transdniestrian representatives publicly joining their Moldovan counterparts, with full media coverage. During the pre-match reception, Moldovan and Transdniestrian leaders, as well as officials from the Irish Football Association, renewed their commitment to mutually beneficial social and cultural exchanges around conflict resolution and development. That the members of the Moldovan football team were drawn from each side of the conflict (as with the Northern Ireland team) was alluded to "as it should be" by leaders from both sides. It was pointed out that such collaboration in sport was an indicator of the possibilities in other areas.

MICOM and the JCDC were also able to facilitate the needs of the two Foreign and Commonwealth Office representatives by bringing together a suitably representative delegation from both Transdniestria and Moldova to meet with them. The Ukrainian Consul, Evghenii Levitsky making his consulate office in Chisinau available, hosted jointly with MICOM two receptions and informal meetings. At these meetings, government officials and the Foreign and Commonwealth Office representatives shared thoughts and ideas with different levels of leadership about the regional crisis, the prevailing circumstances and how these might be dealt with.

Separate from the football-related activities, MICOM and the JCDC had no difficulty undertaking an extensive series of consultative and follow-up meetings, in both Moldova and Transdniestria, with the various levels of leadership, governmental and non-governmental, which had been represented at Albena II. Nor did the prevailing tensions hinder the further development of the JCDC's forthcoming programme. For example, Transdniestrian leaders readily committed themselves to the idea of an inter-university student seminar to be held in Tiraspol. This JCDC-assisted event, aimed at developing mutually beneficial third-level educational systems, would engage students and faculty staff from Moldova, Transdniestria and Gagauzia.[†] President Smirnov of Transdniestria responded positively to the JCDC request for his permission. (The resulting seminar was very successful and was attended by government officials and parliamentarians.)

Such support from governmental authorities for collaborative Moldovan/Transdniestrian activities, despite the prevailing circumstances, was undoubtedly due in large part to the confidence in MICOM and the JCDC which had been built up over the years within the conflict resolution process. This confidence had also helped made it possible for NGOs, local government and inter-government bodies – mayors, heads of local administration and the Joint Control Commission – to engage with each other publicly and productively at the football match and in subsequent discussions.

The MICOM/JCDC partnership had demonstrated, despite political instability, its capacity for constructive networking within and across the security zone separating Moldova from Transdniestria, and across Moldova's international borders.

---

† Gagauzia is an autonomous region within Moldova. The Gagauz struggled for their independence during the same period as Transdniestria, but restraint exercised by both the Moldovans and the Gaugauz resulted in less than 10 deaths. Productive discussions between the Moldovan and Gagauz leaders resulted, in 1995, in a special ethnic-territorial autonomy being agreed for the Gagauz within Moldova.

Local authorities enter the equation: Albena III

The third seminar at Albena, organised by the JCDC and MICOM, was held between 19-26 September 1999. Again funded by DfID, its stated theme was 'Living with Conflict – the Role of Local Authorities'. Recognising that the worst effects of a collapsed economic system, aggravated by the inability to resolve the conflict between Moldova and Transdniestria, were being felt most acutely by those living in villages and towns along the conflict interface, the seminar was an attempt to provide local authorities from this interface with an opportunity to address those needs which could only be dealt with in collaboration with other levels of leadership.

However, although the primary aim of the seminar was to facilitate local authority-based collaborative self-help action among the participants through an identification of shared problems and related needs, this aim was broadened when the Moldovan and Transdniestrian governmental Expert Groups, supported by the OSCE, expressed the wish at the last minute to participate. They were acting in response to more positive national and regional circumstances (largely relating to the situation in Kosovo).

Accordingly, the seminar embraced local authority representatives (mayors) from areas up to 300 miles apart, representatives of the Moldovan and Transdniestrian Expert Groups, members of the Joint Control Commission, the OSCE and Ukrainian mediating ambassadors, parliamentarians, business people, and representatives of NGOs, students and women's groups. Also attending were a number of local authority representatives from all sides of the political divide in Northern Ireland, brought together by Ulster Unionist Party member Chris McGimpsey. The 60 participants included MICOM's facilitation team, as well as invited specialists and speakers.

The seminar was divided into two strands:

In Strand 1 representatives of local authorities spread themselves across all working groups, enabling mayors to work with the other participants on concerns relevant to local needs. Plenary reports from these groups stimulated lively debate surrounding economic, cultural and political issues. Cross-fertilisation of ensuing ideas and plans followed. Ultimately, work focused on how these might be dealt with by those local and central government authorities and NGOs represented at the seminar working independently or collaboratively on their return.

In Strand 2 the Expert Groups and Mediators engaged intensively, identifying areas of work to be taken forward. A member of MICOM was called into their penultimate session as an observer. A report of the outcomes was delivered to a Strand 1 plenary by the OSCE Mediator.

Both strands mixed socially during free time and at meals (one such social occasion being the celebration of Camplisson's 71st birthday). Formal and informal links enhanced complementarity between both processes while informing the work of both strands.

Working alongside the other participants in the various settings were the Northern Ireland local government representatives. Their input was pertinent to the Moldovan and Transdniestrian participants' description of their current situation. The Northern Ireland speakers asked the Moldovans and Transdniestrians whether it was possible or conceivable that their conflict, like that in Northern Ireland, could continue unresolved for 30 years, and whether they wanted to prevent this from happening.

Significantly, one of the Northern Irish panel stated that his own political party had been swept along, often against better judgement, by historical, cultural and other influences, such as innate prejudice. "Our opponents", he remarked, "had set traps which we, *knowingly*, walked into." Such comments were a clear indication that self-defeating policies and actions were now being recognised by both sides in Northern Ireland after 30 years, and this new awareness was helping people to move away from that which was self-defeating towards collaboration.

The confidence and trust of the Moldovan and Transdniestria adversaries in the MICOM/JCDC facilitators, built up over the years, was used to good effect in the workshops focusing on security. The two representatives of the Joint Control Commission, one Moldovan, the other Transdniestrian, had initially worked together in a special interest working group. However, when reporting back to plenary, the way in which one side reported was openly attacked by the other as a distortion of what had been agreed in the group setting. MICOM was subsequently asked to intervene by members of the JCDC after they had failed to induce both representatives to work again in the same group. MICOM was able to persuade them to come together, and from this they brought forward an agreed set of proposals.

Once again, the wealth of ideas which emanated from this third Albena seminar cannot realistically be catalogued here. Suffice to say that all participants agreed that the seminar had been extremely successful and productive, not only in terms of finding new ways of co-operating and collaborating at different levels of leadership, or discussing new possibilities for community development, but of advancing, as one participant put it, "the process of resolving the Moldovan and Transdniestrian conflict."

The local authority representatives in particular emerged from the seminar ready and willing to take a leading role in improving relationships and promoting collaborative action across the Moldovan/Transdniestrian conflict interface. Outputs from the work of the Expert Groups announced to the penultimate plenary session by Ambassador Hill, Head of the OSCE Mission to Moldova, were also positive. Ambassador Hill said that "two to three months of negotiation work had been accomplished in one week." On their return to Moldova the Expert Groups engaged in a three-day seminar working to an agenda developed at Albena. This agenda included the need to agree common economic, security, legal and social space, and borders.

Significant movement was also detected among the Transdniestrian parliamentarians who were present. This, coupled with the positive response of the Expert Groups, could open the way for an inter-parliamentary seminar. (MICOM also sees its efforts to bring parliamentarians and local authorities into the conflict resolution process as a way of forestalling 're-entry' problems for the political leaderships should agreements eventually be signed.)

Finally, and importantly, the Joint Control Commission was asked to consider the recommendations *developed jointly* by their representatives at the seminar. These included ending Bender's seven-year curfew and the establishment of a co-ordinating centre – to deal with policing, courts, etc. – to be run by the Joint Control Commission in association with local authorities and NGOs within the Security Zone.

Joe Camplisson (centre) with members of the JCDC: (from left) Gheorghe Myrzenco, Valentin Romanchiuk, Svetlana Baldencova, Yuri Ataman, Jorj Genunchi, and Evghenii Berdnikov.

Enter the parliamentarians: Albena IV

For the sake of conciseness, this narrative has largely focused on the major events which occurred as part of the Moldovan initiative. In between such events, however, ongoing contact – largely on a daily basis – was maintained between MICOM in Northern Ireland and the JCDC in Moldova – whether by telephone, fax or e-mail. Frequent fact-finding visits to Moldova by Camplisson, Hoffman and Hylton kept them abreast of developments there and assisted in preparations for the various seminars and study visits.

A number of important symposiums were also held in both Northern Ireland and London, at which the MICOM facilitation team explored and debated theory and practice with a number of conflict resolution specialists from the USA, the UK, Germany and elsewhere who had begun to show an increasing interest in MICOM's work.

Camplisson also presented papers on his work in Dagestan, France (Biarritz), Spain (San Sebastian), England and the USA. One conference invite came from Paula Garb, Director of the Program in Citizen Peacebuilding at the University of California, Irvine. At that particular conference, held in June 2000, Camplisson and Yuri Ataman, JCDC, struck up a strong relationship with a group of fellow participants calling themselves Gang Intervention Services, their organisation mostly comprising former Los Angeles gang members. All parties found they had much in common: the violence which had impacted upon their respective communities; the generational nature of that violence; the social and economic problems which fed into it; and even the drug problem, which was rampant and largely out of control in LA but slowly raising its ugly spectre in Northern Ireland and Moldova.

(As a direct result of this encounter a group from Gang Intervention Services visited Belfast in December 2000 to share experiences and debate issues, in what proved to be an extremely valuable exchange.† That visit also saw the LA group make a highly productive link-up with a Belfast and Dublin-based group, Seeds of Hope, comprising both Republican and Loyalist ex-prisoners.)

For their part, the JCDC had been active outside Moldova, and were frequently asked to give advice and assistance to NGOs in neighbouring countries. Norbert Ropers, Director of the Berghof Centre for Constructive Conflict Management, Berlin, involved the JCDC in a series of intra-regional exchanges with others engaged in indigenous approaches to peace-building.

However, on a less positive note, one of the most time-consuming tasks

---

† An account of the visit is given in *Catalysts for Change*, Michael Hall, Island Pamphlets No. 34, Island Publications, Belfast, 2001.

undertaken by MICOM had been one which would be only too familiar to many NGOs – the seemingly unending effort needed, in both man-hours and paperwork, to secure core and programme funding. Constant uncertainty over funding greatly hampered the ability of MICOM and the JCDC to implement their programmes. A major seminar to be held at Vadul-Voda in July 1998, for example, was repeatedly postponed and finally had to be cancelled. Lack of funding had even threatened to substantially curtail the scope of Albena III, and at one stage its cancellation too had seemed possible.

This problem did not apply solely to programme funding, for MICOM has existed without core funding since December 1999, when C S Mott funding ceased.[†] Lack of funding also impacted upon MICOM's plans to hold a fourth seminar at Albena. Extensive planning and preparatory work was undertaken, but the proposed seminar had to be repeatedly cancelled when no funds could be secured. Funding was eventually made available, however, and the seminar was duly scheduled to take place between 9–16 September 2001.

The initial purpose of Albena IV was to assist Moldovan and Transdniestrian parliamentarians in two primary tasks: the development of collaborative inter-governmental/parliamentary action, and to prepare them for the ratification and implementation of any agreements which might be reached in the OSCE-mediated negotiation process. This purpose was to be realised by engaging members of the Moldovan and Transdniestrian Parliamentary Commissions (which had been set up to assist in the search for solutions to the Moldovan/Transdniestrian issue), parliamentarians from both sides of the political divide in Northern Ireland, as well as representatives from various levels of leadership (government, local authority and NGO) within Moldova, Transdniestria and Gagauzia, in a shared training/study programme facilitated by specialists.[††]

However, two separate sets of circumstances threatened postponement of the seminar. In Moldova, a deepening political crisis led to the Transdniestrian authorities pulling out of all contacts with Moldova, including attendance at the seminar. In Northern Ireland a serious outbreak of Loyalist paramilitary feuding (which saw seven people killed and over 200 families evicted from their homes), along with deepening divisions within Unionism, likewise prevented local councillors and all but one parliamentarian from leaving their constituencies to attend. In the event, the seminar went ahead – albeit with a changed programme – largely because of the encouragement the organisers received from the Moldovan governmental authorities, the continuing commitment

---

† Camplisson was fortunate to receive much needed voluntary assistance from accountant Anne-Marie McCluskey, and MICOM Executive member Ian Bell.

†† They included: David Bremner, International Alert and the Institute for Conflict Analysis and Resolution, George Mason University; Rachelle Gray, Trinity Western University, Vancouver; Dr Diana Francis, Chair of the Committee for Conflict Transformation and Support; Dr Kendra Kenyon, San Diego State University; Hugh Pidgeon, Ashridge Business College, Hertfordshire.

expressed by Ambassador William Hill (the OSCE Head of Mission), and the ability of the JCDC, at short notice, to get meaningful replacements from Transdniestria (including NGO representatives who were not under the same constraints as their political colleagues) and Gagauzia.

At the commencement of the seminar Diana Francis, one of the facilitators, proposed a number of 'ground rules', which included: respect for all participants and contributions, listening and paying attention to others, speaking in turn, keeping/sharing time, and remembering the importance of confidentiality. Barney McCaughey, seminar co-director, outlined the programme of work, indicating that much of it would take the form of a 'SWOT analysis' (that is, focusing on Strengths, Weaknesses, Opportunities and Threats).

The main work of the seminar began with a plenary session during which selected speakers provided an overview of the current situation in Moldova, Transdniestria, Gagauzia and Northern Ireland, as seen from four differing perspectives: parliamentarians/government officials, local authorities, NGOs, and others. The participants then divided into smaller groups where they were able to share experiences, exchange lessons learned and begin generating ideas for improvement. Facilitators assisted by keeping the discussion focused and as objective as possible. At a reconvened plenary session a report was presented of each group's findings, conclusions and recommendations.

Another plenary involved a panel of political and civic representatives from Northern Ireland and Great Britain responding to the Moldovan and Transdniestrian SWOT analyses by drawing upon their own experiences. Another plenary discussed priority issues for further development, following which the seminar participants again divided into special interest groups to work on these issues. Each group comprised a mixture of the different categories – parliamentarians, government officials, local authority representatives, NGOs, students, etc. Facilitators were assigned to the various groups according to their areas of knowledge and expertise. Participants from Great Britain and Northern Ireland also joined each of the groups, freely exchanging ideas, experiences and lessons learned. Together they analysed their present situations, and began to generate and further develop ideas for improvement.

The commitment shown by many of the participants was encouraging, some working long into the night making notes in preparation for the next day's workshop. In response to this enthusiasm a supplementary training session was arranged, taking the form of an exercise in 'dialogue and shared analysis', which elicited a very positive response from participants.

In the final workshops participants focused on the lessons learned and discussed ideas and plans for future actions utilising their seminar experience, with a view to developing and implementing these and moving forward upon their return home. At the final plenary sessions the workshop outcomes were shared with the other participants, areas of joint interest and action were explored, and conclusions on the way ahead were drawn.

t was the general consensus of the seminar participants that they had gained much from the experience, in particular the Moldovan parliamentarians, who expressed the view that Albena IV had provided them with an excellent forum for discussion, sharing, analysis, learning and developing ideas. They had also gained a fuller understanding of their responsibilities and authority, and of the potential for complementarity with other levels of leadership engaged in the processes of negotiation and conflict resolution.

All participants were able to draw from lessons learned in Northern Ireland in attempting to preserve the integrity of democratic leadership and processes during thirty years of violent conflict and a complex peace process. All participants also further developed their ability to engage in productive relations with different levels of leadership – parliamentarians, government officials, local authorities, NGOs and others.

Importantly, members of the Moldovan Parliamentary Commission gained valuable insights into the work of the JCDC, and its desire to be of assistance to them and their Transdniestrian counterparts. Despite the absence of Transdniestrian parliamentarians the Moldovan parliamentarians engaged productively with other levels of Transdniestrian leadership.

The Gagauz parliament, with its regional autonomy, could have an important role to play in Moldovan-Transdniestrian relationship building. The input of the Gagauz representatives during the seminar was particularly valuable, and good relationships were established between the Gagauz representatives, Moldovan parliamentarians and the different levels of Transdniestrian leadership present, which would hopefully stand them in good stead for entering into collaborative dialogue. Likewise, local authority representatives and NGOs worked in small groups on shared concerns with parliamentarians, establishing productive working relationships between different levels of leadership, furthering the prospects of continuing rapprochement when they returned to Moldova.

One anecdote might give some indication of the positive dynamic of the seminar. One of the four Moldovan governmental representatives initially brought a hostile reserve in her engagement with seminar facilitation and other forms of authority present, including the OSCE, and in this she was sometimes supported by her colleagues. Accusations of partiality and manipulation persisted until the fourth day of the seminar. However, following an intensive examination of the concerns voiced, mistrust was dispelled and an amicable working relationship established. By the conclusion of the seminar all members of the Moldovan Parliamentary Commission praised the professionalism and impartiality of the facilitators and expressed their gratitude for what they had gained from the seminar.

The JCDC programme gathers momentum

The JCDC are now working extensively at all levels of leadership throughout the 'three regions' (Moldova, Transdniestria and Gagauzia). Their current (2002) programme – despite funding uncertainties – includes:

- A seminar looking at the role of women in leadership – in political, economic and social life – involving the three regions.
- A continuation of work already commenced with youth, attempting to build a youth network embracing the three regions.
- A seminar focusing on the experiences of national minorities from the three regions.
- A pilot programme involving five villages from Moldova and five from Transdniestria for the purpose of sharing information. (At the moment there is a great shortage of information; the radio network in many villages does not work properly and most people cannot afford to subscribe to newspapers.)
- Linked in with the above is a scheme called 'Leading Lights', aimed at helping the JCDC identify the right people who could not only tell them what is going on in the regions, but could act as a conduit for the spread of information, provide services to local NGOs and community leaders, and assist the implementation and monitoring of JCDC programmes.
- A proposal, which was supported by the OSCE, for the convening of informal meetings with members of the Governmental Expert Groups, Parliamentary Commissions, the Joint Control Commission, and international experts.

Comments made at a youth seminar, held in the town of Baltsi, revealed to the JCDC that an optimism still resided within the new generation:

> Let's look at each other not through the distorted TV programmes and political contradictions but from the point of view of neighbours who wish changes for the best.

> We should recognise the nature of the problem. This conflict exists because our leaders are looking at their actions through the prism of their own interests.

> The recent disaster (11 September 2001 terrorist attacks on the USA) should make all of us think carefully about the global issues which threaten our civilisation and our planet. The spectrum of problems is wide – ecological pollution, wars, AIDS, hunger, etc. But although these are global problems we can start their resolution from the places where we live.

The youth must stay united; we are the future leaders and we should learn to avoid the mistakes of the previous generations.

Because I am a citizen and patriot I cannot look calmly at what is happening to my country. I love my Motherland. I love the Earth. I love people. This is all about our pain.

There are many problems which concern each one of us, yet we wait for those in positions of authority to solve these things alone. That is wrong; we should *all* participate to the best of our capabilities in the resolution of these problems, especially at this very difficult time.

I do not think our top economic-political élites want resolution of the conflict; I think it will be left to ordinary people to find a resolution themselves.

Sharing information and experiences at this seminar with people like myself has left me much wiser. Now it all depends on me how I am going to use this new knowledge in practice.

The Baltsi seminar confirmed to the JCDC that youth NGOs were ready to communicate and co-operate, and to implement joint programmes which could contribute to a better informed population, to the overcoming of the existing stereotypes of 'enemies', and the eventual bringing together of the different sides in a spirit of tolerance. The youth also displayed their interest in taking a pro-active position with regard to political issues such as active participation in the political life of the state, and informing those in authority about the opinions of youth on issues of concern.

Furthermore, although the series of youth seminars also involved local authority representatives and the OSCE, the youth leaders were anxious to widen their engagement even further, proposing: "a seminar on the theme 'the Moldovan/Transdniestrian conflict', with the participation in it of the leadership of Moldova, Transdniestria, the OSCE Mission and foreign Mediators."

The JCDC is a member of a new network of NGOs working within the CIS (Commonwealth of Independent States) – 'The Working Group of NGOs from CIS on prevention and resolution of conflicts'. This network consists of three sub-networks: the Central Asia network, the Caucasian network, and the Western network which includes Moldova, Ukraine and Belorussia. In 2002 the JCDC was elected Co-ordinator of the Western Group, and one of their tasks is to try and involve NGOs from Central European countries in the network: Romania, Poland, Hungary and perhaps Serbia. It is evident that the expertise which the members of the JCDC have acquired while working at the interface of their own conflict will be increasingly put to productive use well outside the borders of Moldova and Transdniestria.

Postscript

In Moldova unemployment remains high with little investment in the economy, over 60% of which falls within the 'black' or 'grey' categories. Some superficial signs of prosperity may be attributed to the sizeable remittances coming from expatriate workers: almost one quarter of the population now work outside the country.

In Transdniestria at the end of January 2002 the Russian company ITERA ceased supplying gas to the steel works and other industries because of Transdniestria's failure to pay mounting debt. This could seriously impact upon all aspects of life in Transdniestria.

The gas problem is linked to another issue. Under an agreement reached in Istanbul – with regard to the withdrawal of the Russian 14th Army from Transdniestria – the Russians were to remove their heavy equipment, reduce the number of soldiers and begin the destruction of ammunition. A separate agreement was also signed whereby Russia would pay Transdniestria for some of the removed equipment, and with this money Transdniestria would pay its gas debt. At first the removal of the munitions proceeded without incident but in December 2001 the Transdniestrians placed concrete blocks on the railway line used to transport the munitions, giving as one of their reasons for doing so that Russia was not paying up in time. A serious rift has now developed between Transdniestria and Russia. This dramatic change in relationships – for Transdniestria had greatly relied on tacit if not direct Russian support – has in turn damaged relations between Transdniestria and Moldova, as the former are blaming Moldova for this turnaround in their political fortunes.

In both Moldova and Transdniestria people's initial fears regarding their cultural identities would appear to have been largely sidelined by the more immediate concerns of everyday living. Nevertheless, when, in December 2001, the Minister of Education in Moldova issued a decree making the teaching of Russian compulsory in all Moldovan schools – from the second form upwards – it sparked off street demonstrations[†] organised by the pro-

---

† In 1998, C S Mott Foundation commissioned an evaluation of MICOM's work by CDR Associates, USA. Their report, while extremely positive, nevertheless felt that MICOM had failed to recognize that "the situation in Moldova and Transdniestria is not currently an identity-based conflict." MICOM would contend, however, that as all attempts to reach a negotiated settlement, despite the best efforts of highly motivated and skilled mediators, had proven abortive, the underlying reasons behind the frequent impasses frustrating collaboration at inter-governmental level needed to be examined in depth. If the roots of the problem were solely political or power-based – and did *not* embrace an identity-related dimension – one might have hoped for greater movement towards a compromise accommodation, especially when the economic situation in both Moldova and Transdniestria provided a compelling incentive for both sides to reach such an accommodation. These street demonstrations (although supported by only a minority of the population) reveal that identity-

Romanian Christian Democratic People's Party. Transdniestria points to this as a justification of their fear of unification with Romania, and contend that Moldova should make Russian a recognised second language of the state.

Although there are no negotiations currently taking place between the two sides the members of the JCDC are not disheartened, as Evghenii Berdnikov remarked:

> We faced a far more complicated situation in '92, and I believe people will now be wise enough to turn way from violent conflict. I think we should continue to work with members of the two parliaments because an agreement will eventually be reached.

In April 2002, Camplisson, Hylton and Hoffman – facilitated by the JCDC – met with the OSCE, the US Ambassador and all levels of governmental leadership in Moldova and Transdniestria. The general mood was pessimistic; at presidential and Expert Group[†] level there was no will to engage with one another. Despite this, both Parliamentary Commissions remain willing to come to Northern Ireland later in the year for a series of MICOM workshops. On his return from Moldova, Camplisson commented:

> I think both sides are on the threshold of something new. The crisis involving the gas supply has brought matters to a head. I believe that the realities are now on the table for all to see, not only with respect to Moldova and Transdniestria, but there is now a greater clarity as to the way in which Russian, Ukrainian and Romanian concerns can either hinder or advance the search for resolution. The question is: can they use their awareness of this reality – Russia, Ukraine and Romania as well as the Moldovan/Transdniestrian protagonists – to move together into something much more positive? I think they can.
>
> If the two Parliamentary Commissions come to Northern Ireland as planned, they have agreed that their programme will include a workshop in which they will engage in a shared analysis. If this proves to be productive it might encourage a much deeper involvement, by other levels of leadership, in the conflict resolution process.

---

related issues remain, even if under the surface. Indeed, at Albena II the MICOM facilitators were surprised by the persistence with which the language issue was raised as a problem. History has provided ample evidence that as long as identity-needs remained unsatisfied, even if they are temporarily sidelined by other needs, they could readily rise to the surface again. MICOM's fear is that if such needs are not addressed now, then a future generation of Moldovans and Transdniestrians could find themselves burdened with a tragic renewal of violence.

† The Expert Groups changed their name to Expert Commissions in the second half of 2000.

Part 2

Reflections

Are there lessons to be drawn?

MICOM's involvement in Moldova is now in its tenth year, and while there is no doubting the trust which MICOM and the JCDC have established at all levels of leadership in Moldova and Transdniestria, and no doubting the constructive role which both organisations have played in the rebuilding of civil society, progress towards a resolution of the Moldovan/Transdniestrian conflict has been painfully slow. Is it realistic then for MICOM and the JCDC to hope that lessons drawn from their experience can prove valuable to those confronting deep-rooted, identity-related conflicts elsewhere in the world?

At one of the MICOM symposiums – bringing together the MICOM facilitation team with interested conflict resolution scholars and practitioners from different countries – Jonathan Cohen (Director, Conciliation Resources, London) reminded the participants that the Moldovan/Transdniestrian conflict had arisen at the same time as other conflicts in the former Soviet Union, most of which had also experienced some degree of violence and intransigence but which were in a far less constructive situation – such as Nagorno-Karabakh, Tajikistan, Georgia/Abkhazia, Georgia/Ossetia. And then there had been the tragic situation in the Balkans. So although the Moldovan situation might be frustrating, Cohen felt that MICOM's intervention had been part of a process which had undoubtedly prevented the degree of intractability seen in those other conflicts.

MICOM believes that, even if movement towards conflict resolution in Moldova has not gone beyond a shared rejection of the military option and an acceptance of the need to pursue a 'win-win' outcome, present methods of confronting identity-related, ethnic or religious conflicts around the world are failing in their objective, despite the best of intentions, immense material resources and even overwhelming military strength directed at this task by international organisations. Many experts in the field of conflict resolution, for example, believe that the Dayton Accord for Bosnia was basically a 'holding operation', leaving ethnic hatreds still simmering below the surface. And while the use of NATO air power might have contained the immediate humanitarian crisis in Kosovo, conflict resolution remains elusive. Furthermore, as this book goes to press, the Israeli/Palestinian 'peace process' lies in tatters, with an escalating death toll. Given this reality, the case has been made for a need for an alternative way of tackling deep-rooted, identity-related violent conflict.

But what would such an alternative entail? In any situation of deep-rooted ethnic or religious conflict, with the world's media focusing on the daily plight of the victims – the refugees, the dispossessed, the bereaved – the pressure upon the international community would be for a speedy response.

An approach which took years to begin to bear fruit – such as MICOM's ten-year efforts in Moldova – would be clearly unrealistic. Nevertheless, the *reality* is that a 'quick-fix' solution, *without* conflict resolution, might only ensure the resurgence of the conflict a generation later in all its former intensity.

In Moldova, it has been shown that a needs-based conflict resolution process has complemented the OSCE-mediated negotiation process. In the light of this, the UN and OSCE might usefully, in situations of identity-related violent conflict, be open to the idea of incorporating *three separate but complementary* forms of intervention:

- a team to mediate negotiations aimed at *conflict containment/management*, addressing immediate survival needs;
- an independent team to facilitate *conflict resolution* attempts, addressing the root causes of the conflict and long-term needs;
- an independent team to introduce and facilitate a *community development* strategy embracing all levels of leadership, aimed at creating a peaceful, prosperous society.

(If the international community failed to overcome hostility to peaceful third-party intervention, its only option might be military force in order to attain humanitarian objectives.)

If these teams were able to work together in a complementary manner they would be more likely to achieve a satisfactory outcome. This would require a high degree of awareness of, and sensitivity to, each other's process requirements. In particular, the team engaged in mediated negotiations would need to proceed in such a manner that any 'settlement' they helped bring about kept the door open for movement towards conflict resolution. For its part, the conflict resolution team would have to ensure, as far as possible, that the process of analysis did not frustrate the process of negotiations.

An effective conflict resolution process could only proceed when it received the authority to do so by the parties to the conflict. Furthermore, there might be concerns among some of the protagonists that they would not be accorded parity of esteem by their adversaries or the mediator. If the conflict resolution facilitation team, however, comprised individuals who were known to have successfully established parity of esteem between protagonists in similar circumstances elsewhere, these barriers might be overcome.

The facilitation of a community development strategy (which MICOM believes is essential to any attempt at conflict resolution) by a suitably qualified external team would be enhanced by this team working alongside an indigenous group able to act as an 'internal third party' (and accepted as such by the main protagonists). Depending on the circumstances, such a group might or might not exist. It might be possible, however, to call upon the assistance of similar groups elsewhere in the region to stimulate the development of such a group. (The JCDC, for example, is increasingly establishing productive relationships with similar bodies outside the borders of Moldova/Transdniestria, who are hoping to learn from the JCDC's experiences.)

The problems, but also the opportunities, attendant upon two different processes working alongside one another were highlighted by the JCDC's chairman, Yuri Ataman:

> An organisation like the OSCE will inevitably direct most of its efforts into reaching a political solution, and this is more likely to be achieved through a power-bargaining approach, in which the opposing sides attempt to use their political, economic, international, strategic and military might to 'persuade' the other side to accept their proposals. There are a number of obvious problems with such an approach: it invariably implies that one side 'wins' and the other 'loses'; any short-term political agreement may still leave the underlying problems unresolved; the negotiations are largely dependent on whatever political parties happen to be in power at the time, and political changes can derail the process; and, finally, the negotiations usually only involve the top level leadership.
>
> On the other hand, a conflict resolution process, such as based on Basic Human Needs Theory, is directed at the resolution of the problems which lie at the core of the conflict, and has as its goal a 'win-win' outcome. It also works with *all* levels of leadership.
>
> While each process poses difficulties for the other, the Moldovan experience has shown that the OSCE *has* been able to accept the conflict resolution process as complementary to its own. The conflict resolution process, for example, may indirectly enhance the negotiation process by assisting the sides to move away from simply throwing proposals onto the table and pushing for them to be accepted to concentrating on the real underlying problems and the search for a solution. For its part, the conflict resolution process might be able to establish itself more solidly in the breathing space provided by a short-term political agreement – such as a ceasefire or transitional agreement. Indeed, even if, after an assisted analysis, the sides reach a common understanding of the problem and have a common vision of their future, they will still have to negotiate ways to translate that vision into reality – the conflict resolution process alone might not suffice.

If the problems posed by two such seemingly incompatible processes working together can be satisfactorily addressed, and a realistic alternative designed which is found to be acceptable, and workable, by the international community, then perhaps an important step forward will have been taken in helping humankind confront one of its most pressing problems – that of deep-rooted, identity-related violent conflict.

Overview: *Joe Camplisson*

The cost of violent ethnic, religious, and identity-related conflict in the 20th century was measured in millions of deaths and widespread devastation of the social and physical environment. With the spin-off from such conflict becoming increasingly global it is imperative, even for the survival of the human species, that the international community undertakes a fundamental reassessment of the strategies it has been utilising in its response. These strategies could be described as largely 'power-based' approaches, in that they identify these conflicts as power struggles, and see the solution in conflict containment.

History has shown, however, that attempts at containment of deep-rooted violent conflict have been, in the main, often only temporary in nature, and have been costly in human, social, political, economic and environmental/ecological terms. In the current Middle East crisis, this deeply flawed approach only serves to compound the self-defeating strategies already being pursued by the main protagonists. Unable to have cognisance of the real causes of conflict, such forms of intervention have shown themselves to be often detrimental to the search for a lasting solution: *the resolution of the conflict.*

Among those engaged in the study of the causes of deep-rooted violent conflicts there is a growing acceptance of the existence of a 'needs paradigm', as described by Burton, and an acknowledgement that perhaps it is only a successful conflict resolution process which can realistically deliver needs satisfaction.

That a significant difference exists between a 'power-based' approach and a 'conflict resolution' approach is readily discernible even in the concepts and language used by each. Within a *power-based* approach there might be talk of 'conflict management/containment/transformation', 'mediated negotiations', 'compromise solutions', 'agreements guaranteed by third parties', 'negotiating positions determined by the amount of power wielded' and so on. Within a *conflict resolution* approach talk is centred around 'a problem-solving process', 'assisted analysis', 'identity-related needs', 'a win-win outcome', 'a collaborative search for needs satisfiers', 'parity of esteem' and so on.

Of course, conflict resolution theorists and practitioners do not have a shared definition of conflict resolution or the philosophy underpinning their practice. The conflict resolution approach utilised by MICOM is specifically based on John Burton's Basic Human Needs Theory. This holds that where the satisfaction of deep-rooted, identity-related needs is frustrated or denied violent conflict is likely to ensue and pass from generation to generation. It also holds that only *resolution* of such conflict – rather than its *containment* – will suffice, and that it will only be resolved when those needs are satisfied.

Societies engulfed by deep-rooted, identity-related conflict often simultaneously face severe social and economic disruption. Moldova and Transdniestria not only experienced war – arising, in part, from *the manner of pursuit* of the satisfaction of identity-related needs – but also severe problems – socio-economic, political, cultural and technical – surrounding the development of an independent state, civil society and a viable plural democracy. MICOM's approach embraces *all* these elements, largely because its conflict resolution process is accommodated within an overarching community development strategy, which engages with all levels of leadership, from village to governmental.

Community development as understood and introduced into Moldova by MICOM is an instrument of change. It is a professionally-assisted analytical process aimed at the identification and addressing of real needs within an 'indirect' approach to community development. This does not establish organisations or projects, but acts in a catalytic way to encourage *self-help development*. On a practical level, the community development strategy is essentially facilitated experiential learning within a context and focused on participants' developmental needs – personal, social and specialist – relative to their respective functions. Outcomes, through participants, feed into and impact positively upon social, economic, political and cultural systems.

MICOM's conflict resolution process is accommodated within, and complemented by, this community development process. Alongside the workshops involving the governmental Expert Groups, parliamentarians and others, the normalisation of relationships between Moldova and Transdniestria is also fostered. This promotes the establishment of self-sustaining and mutually beneficial collaborative activities between the conflicting governments, between people, and between people and government. As this book has shown, MICOM and the JCDC have been successfully engaged at *all* levels of leadership – both *within* and *between* Moldova and Transdniestria – promoting conciliation at the conflict interface while generating and sustaining movement towards the resolution of conflict.

Despite its deep philosophical concerns regarding the efficacy of power-based interventions, MICOM acknowledges that the international community is motivated by a genuine desire to prevent human suffering. It has striven, therefore, to develop a complementarity between the two approaches, in the hope that this will prove mutually beneficial. The reader will have noted the close co-operation which has been established between the conflict resolution process and the mediating ambassadors of the OSCE, Russia and Ukraine, who are endeavouring to work towards a negotiated settlement of the Moldovan/Transdniestrian conflict. Indeed, for some scholars and practitioners in the field of international relations and conflict resolution this has been the most significant outcome of MICOM's work.

However, the two processes can also create problems for one another, and in this lies their seeming incompatibility. If, for example, in Moldova the negotiation process yielded a compromise agreement on the status of Transdniestria this could institutionalise those divisions brought about by the unresolved conflict, which in its turn could perpetuate the danger of recurring violence. This status would have to be proposed by a third party, one side or the other. It is unlikely, therefore, to enjoy ownership in equal measure by both sides and would need external guarantors for its protection. If, on the other hand, this end product was the outcome of a successful conflict resolution process, developed by both sides as that which satisfies their own and each other's needs – which, by being denied or frustrated, had given rise to the conflict – it is more likely to be self-sustaining.

Likewise, pushing the analysis within the conflict resolution process can slow up and frustrate the process of negotiation because negotiations are concerned with reaching a compromise over contentious issues rather than focusing on *why* those issues are on the table, as is the case in the conflict resolution process. In other words, mediated negotiations are issue-centred; in a conflict resolution process the same issues are used to push the analysis.

However, through the development and maintenance of complementarity between both processes, it should be possible to ensure continuing movement towards conflict resolution following a negotiated settlement of the dispute. But such complementarity is only possible where the aim of the mediated settlement is partly to advance movement towards conflict resolution. In the Moldovan situation there has been an increasingly shared understanding between the OSCE, the international Mediators and MICOM in this regard.

MICOM's local partner, the JCDC, continues to advance, through the community development and conflict resolution strategy at all levels of society in Moldova, Transdniestria and Gagauzia, this shared objective. Significantly, the JCDC is being called upon to share its experiences with others in the region, and its work is being followed with great interest – and with great hope – by many scholars and practitioners in the field of conflict resolution.

Astro-physicist Stephen Hawking predicts an end to all life forms on Earth before the end of this millennium. If this gloomy assessment is not to be proven accurate humanity must develop harmony with the ecosystem and the environment, social and physical, and look at the world anew: without ideological, nationalistic or cultural fixations; as one socio-economic and political space the ownership of which is shared by everyone; and as a place where a concern for dignity and parity of esteem determines all relationships.

As a first step we need to approach deep-rooted, identity-related violent conflict with new ways of thinking, recognising and rejecting the self-defeating nature of the military option, and seeing such conflict as a shared problem which can be solved through assisted analysis. A conflict resolution process underpinned by Basic Human Needs, with its 'win-win' philosophy, could be an essential aid, as Burton indicates, to the survival of the human race.

A personal view: *Michael Hall*

My initial willingness to be drawn into an association with MICOM was motivated more by the humanitarian precepts underpinning its work than by any sudden conversion to the conflict resolution process MICOM was advocating. For although the core elements of Basic Human Needs Theory were attractive from a commonsense point of view, the conflict resolution process which was derived from it seemed heavily dependent on a positive engagement with three categories of people I have always viewed with much scepticism: politicians, extremists and 'specialists'.

On the political level I was somewhat concerned that, according to Camplisson, conflict resolution could, ultimately, only be delivered by those in positions of responsibility and power – in particular, the political leadership of a people or a country. Having spent 30 years feeling totally frustrated by the inability of Northern Ireland's politicians to provide positive leadership, I found it difficult to share Camplisson's faith in the willingness, let alone the capacity, of political leaders to move forward productively in such a manner. Even Northern Ireland's present power-sharing Assembly and Executive is riven with the brinkmanship and game-playing that has become second-nature to our politicians, of all ideological hues.

Over the 30 years I had also watched helplessly while those at 'the extremes' bequeathed a bloody legacy of butchery and grief to the communities all around me. (For the sake of argument, I am restricting the label of 'extremist' to those who resort to violence in pursuit of their goals, although I am well aware that an equally dangerous extremism also exists within political parties, religious groupings and the security establishment.) Whilst accepting that some of those extremists certainly fitted into Camplisson's category of individuals whose deep-rooted, identity-related needs had been thwarted or denied – many Irish Nationalists are clearly driven by a sense of lost nationhood, and many Ulster Loyalists are motivated by a fear of impending cultural disintegration – I had encountered many others whose primary identification seemed to be with the *struggle itself* – not its supposed objective.

When conflict resolution theorists and practitioners talk, as Camplisson does, of "involving the extremes in the resolution of the conflict", I believe that they need to be certain that the particular extremists they are dealing with *do actually represent* the deep-rooted, identity-related needs of communities in conflict, and are not motivated by *other* needs,[†] ones which fall neither within their responsibility nor their competence to address.

---

†   It is quite evident that in many different arenas of conflict there exist political parties who have a

Finally, Camplisson believes that it is only a team of outside specialists, acting as a neutral, external 'third party', who can hope to facilitate movement towards conflict resolution between warring parties, as these parties are invariably too close to the problem to be able to step back from it without assistance. My difficulty again is that my experience of the numerous conflict resolution 'specialists' and others who have turned their attention to the Northern Ireland conflict over the last 30 years has not been encouraging. For every specialist I met who acted in a genuinely professional manner I encountered self-indulgent others who left me harbouring more suspicions about their personal, organisational[††] or governmental agendas than I care to record here.[†††]

Given such personal difficulties with politicians, extremists and specialists, why then am I such an enthusiastic supporter of MICOM and its work? The answer is that, despite my scepticism, I have repeatedly witnessed the positive impact which MICOM has had upon all three categories. I have heard – to my surprise – local politicians admitting: "What we have been doing has been self-defeating; we need help to move forward." I have worked with members of Republican and Loyalist paramilitary organisations who had a genuine desire to build a peaceful and just society. I have met academics and other specialists who genuinely sought to offer their expertise to communities in conflict, rather than feed off that conflict to advance their own career needs.

MICOM – perhaps because of its non-threatening approach, its obvious concern with humanitarian values, and its absolute insistence that ownership of any process of conflict resolution must always belong to the parties themselves – seems able to elicit the best qualities from the people with whom it engages (*including* politicians, extremists and specialists). I have witnessed – not only in relation to the efforts made by MICOM and the JCDC in Moldova but with

---

vested interest in forestalling resolution, just as there are armed groupings who fear that resolution will endanger lucrative income from drugs or contraband. There are also 'extremists' who were not radicalised by their life circumstances but who become professional revolutionaries through ideological conviction. One can think of Lenin (who developed his theories, not on the factory floor, but in endless debates with fellow middle-class intellectuals) guiding his Bolshevik Party through a systematic destruction of the creative revolutionary achievements of the Russian people – because he imagined that he, rather than they, knew best how to create a new society. A more recent example would be Osama bin Laden, the Saudi-born multimillionaire who purported to speak on behalf of some of the world's dispossessed. Such extremists are certainly able to *articulate* 'the problem', but they don't necessarily *represent* that problem, and are therefore not able to act to resolve it.

†† An example of this occurred a few years ago when a misleading article about Moldova appeared in an influential journal. The author, an academic introduced to those engaged in this self-help initiative, implied exclusive ownership and control (by the organisation he was representing) of the conflict resolution process. It is important that journals cross-reference academic articles describing the author's intervention in current conflict situations. Misrepresentation can often confuse the policy-making community and place self-help organisations, such as the JCDC, at a funding disadvantage.

††† Some of these encounters I have described in *Reinforcing Powerlessness*, Island Pamphlet No. 14, Island Publications, Belfast, 1996.

regard to the relationships MICOM has developed in Northern Ireland – the way in which individuals representing *all* levels of leadership have shown themselves willing to not only engage productively in the conflict resolution process, but to work collectively towards the development of a shared vision.

Although this experience has been extremely encouraging, nevertheless I feel that this book would be greatly negligent if it failed to warn its *primary* audience – those communities who are either experiencing deep-rooted, identity-related violent conflict, or who are fearful of its advent – that when in their desperation they reach out to political leaders, extremists or international specialists to help resolve their conflict, that all these categories of people have the potential – for different reasons and to different degrees – to become part of the problem. To protect themselves against this, communities must endeavour to retain as much ownership as is possible over any processes of political negotiations or conflict resolution which might be put in place, and always be prepared to challenge their composition, agenda or perceived outcomes.

An added safeguard would be to ensure that, as in Moldova, any conflict resolution process was rooted within an all-embracing community development strategy, one which assisted the emergence of indigenous peacemaking organisations, such as the JCDC. Indeed, my hope is that in *any* situation of deep-rooted, identity-related conflict groups will emerge who can act as such 'indigenous peacemakers', and that these groups, guided perhaps by the conflict resolution process as described in this book – a possible 'route map', if you like – can find an indigenous path to the resolution of their conflict.

I accept that this leaves me at variance with Camplisson's strongly held belief that only professional, 'third-party' assistance from outside can effectively facilitate movement towards conflict resolution, and, indeed, in this view he is supported by members of the JCDC, a leading figure commenting: "Without our external support our political leaders might treat us as just one NGO among many – and ignore us." Perhaps that is the reality. However, just as MICOM's community development strategy "acts in a catalytic way to encourage self-help development", my hope is that this 'route map', utilised to best advantage by indigenous peacemakers, could serve in a similarly catalytic manner.

Supplementary Notes

1: Basic Human Needs Theory

- MICOM believes that if a conflict contains significant elements of a deep-rooted, identity-related nature then a process of mediated negotiations (i.e. a 'power-based' process aimed at a compromise settlement) will not by itself bring resolution, and could even leave a legacy of bitterness which will be acted upon by succeeding generations.

- If *resolution* is the ultimate objective, a conflict resolution process must be underpinned and guided by a sound theoretical understanding† of the dynamics of deep-rooted, identity-related conflict, and MICOM believes that John Burton's Basic Human Needs (BHN) theory provides this.

- BHN theory holds that, in order to bring about an end to violent conflict, alternatives have to be found to the use of violence as a means of securing the satisfaction of needs, and the only way to satisfy the needs of *all* the parties to a conflict is to engage the parties in an *assisted analysis* in which all their needs can be identified, and in which the violent strategies employed by all sides to satisfy such needs can be seen for what they invariably are – self-defeating.

- Such an analysis will hopefully lead the parties away from the notion of 'an enemy to be destroyed', into seeing their conflict as 'a shared problem to be solved'.

- In order to resolve such a problem BHN theory holds that one's own needs can only be satisfied if the needs of one's enemy are also satisfied, and consequently each party has a vested interest in satisfying the needs of its enemy.

- The assisted analysis proposed by BHN theory can best be carried out by an independent 'third party' team of conflict resolution expert facilitators.

- In summary, the basic aim of assisted analysis is to facilitate movement towards conflict resolution by bringing parties to the conflict to:
  - accept the conflict as a shared problem which may be solved through collaborative action;
  - reject the notion of victory and pursue the idea of a win-win outcome;
  - engage freely with one another in an exploration of existing options, or the development of new ones;
  - work towards the satisfaction of the needs of all parties – particularly those whose frustration or denial gave rise to the conflict;

2: Possible outline of a conflict resolution workshop

MICOM is hesitant to suggest that there could be a 'blueprint' for an effective conflict resolution (CR) process, as adaptability to individual circumstances is paramount. Furthermore, the development of CR skills and competencies is still in an embryonic state.

---

† A process aimed at an objective such as conflict resolution or conflict containment, if not underpinned by a theory is, in Camplisson's words, "like a headless chicken being led by a rudderless facilitator". He believes that such processes, unfortunately, appear to be the norm rather than the exception in dealing with identity-related violent conflicts.

Nevertheless, the following guidelines might be of value to those seeking to facilitate CR workshops.

- The process would be facilitated by an international team of conflict resolution specialists (acting as a neutral third party), acceptable to all sides.

- Initiation of the CR process is preceded by a series of explanatory meetings with all potential participants to explain the purpose of the process and how it is to be conducted. The CR process can only begin when the various parties to the conflict see a value in committing themselves to an analysis of needs and the underlying causes of their conflict.

- The process is different from that of mediation, political negotiation, or the search for compromise or short-term accommodation. The team's function at all times is to facilitate *movement towards* long-term conflict resolution among the protagonists. To this end, the parties are instead encouraged to approach their conflict as a *shared* problem and to engage in a 'problem-solving' process, the essence of which is always analysis.

- The preliminary, foundation-laying objective is to engage leaders of the protagonists in a 'mapping out of the conflict' – that is, an identification of all those other party leaders who must be brought into the process for it to succeed. Only those with the capacity to deliver resolution of the conflict, and facilitators, should have a role in the CR workshop.

- At commencement, each side states their aspirations and has these aspirations subjected to an assisted self-analysis to ascertain the nature of the conflict, the identity-related needs at its core (including those of one's opponents) and the manner of pursuit of needs satisfaction. The facilitators must not provide this analysis, but assist the participants to focus on the difficult and often painful work of honest, open and thorough exploration.

- Successful assisted analysis would clarify the parties' objectives and thereby assist an exploration of those actions and strategies which either hindered or advanced the satisfaction of their respective needs.

- Thoughts and ideas which might prove to be mutually beneficial and boost confidence in the process and in each other would also be identified and action planned. To this end the parties might look at the experience of other conflicts around the world.

- Ultimately, short and long-term strategies for engendering ongoing *movement towards* conflict resolution might then be agreed upon and set in place.

- In summary, in the shared analysis they:
  - present their perceptions of problems and their related needs, and subject these to in-depth analysis aimed at a shared understanding of causes;
  - listen to the presentations of others and explore how their opponents have sought to satisfy *their* needs and aspirations;
  - assess the self-defeating nature of, or conversely the benefits of, some of their own and their opponents' policies and strategies;
  - identify areas of mutuality;
  - identify areas of conflict;
  - identify impediments to the resolution of their conflict;
  - explore, with the assistance of the facilitators, how such impediments had been, or were being, addressed elsewhere.

- The first indication that *movement towards* conflict resolution is occurring is when the participants agree to undertake their analysis in a *co-operative* way. Meeting together they identify the different needs and aspirations which must be satisfied, and search for means by which this can be achieved.

- Such movement towards conflict resolution begins to be consolidated when the parties reach essential aims within the process: they accept the self-defeating nature of violent strategies; they embrace the idea of searching for a 'win/win' outcome; and they begin a shared search for the satisfaction of all needs – their own and those of their enemy. It is only when this has occurred that the search for solutions surrounding specific issues (problems) should begin. Hitherto, such issues are employed solely as an aid to analysis.

- The process may seek, in some circumstances, to *complement*, rather than compete with, any existing negotiating process. Complementarity, however, is only attainable where parties to the negotiations and their mediators give credence to the process of CR. Gains made in the 'problem-solving' process can then improve the efficacy of any negotiating process.

- Unlike mediated negotiations there is no pressure to find agreements or solutions. The 'problem-solving' process sets no agenda other than that which the participants agree to. This will hopefully compensate for any sense the participants might have that self-analysis is inherently threatening, especially if they engage in such analysis in front of an 'enemy'.

- If, during the problem-solving process, the parties move away from analysis towards issues or areas where agreement *is* possible, discussion surrounding these are transferred to the separate negotiating process. The absence of any expectation to reach political accommodation in the problem-solving process should ensure that it remains available as a trust-building forum should the negotiating process face stalemate.

- Engaging in an assisted self-analysis, for most participants, is a 'step into the unknown', and a high degree of self-confidence is essential, both at individual and at delegation level, if the CR process is to be successful. Participants also require an ability to pursue objectives purposefully within the process. In Moldova/Transdniestria, numerous activities have been initiated *outside* the CR workshops but complementary to them, aimed at building such confidence and ability through personal, communal, political, economic, cultural, structural and institutional development.

3: Facilitation skills

- A facilitator should not *bring* an analysis *to* the participants in the way a mediator might do, but *assist* the participants arrive at their *own* analysis.

- *An ability to listen* is important, as also is the *manner* in which one listens, whereby you provide some indication to those in the room that you are taking what they say seriously, and that you are treating them as genuine interlockers.

- The *ability to foster a conversation* is also important, as is an ability to impart a notion of *critique*, both in asking certain questions, and posing them in ways which challenge what people are saying, not in a manner which is threatening or which belittles them, but which draws them back into the conversation. A form of critique which encourages people to think about the particular positions, values and assumptions that are perhaps unarticulated behind what is being said.

- While traditionally the idea is that the 'third party' facilitator simply oversees the process and the dialogue taking place between the parties – as opposed to becoming a 'participant other' – good facilitation involves the ability to be able to *provide* something to the participants which helps to move the conversation along, but without it being directive – such as feedback, commentary, or making summaries of the discussion to help people focus..

- Being able to make explicit the nature of the contract between facilitator and group is important. As is being sensitive to when the facilitation process itself might change – a stage might be reached, for example, where a bit more commentary and even direction may be deemed necessary for the survival of the process, as long as this does not inhibit the group keeping responsibility and making their own decisions.

Island Pamphlets

Island Pamphlets deal with political, cultural, socio-economic and community issues in Northern Ireland. They average 32 pages and cost **£2.50** each (inclusive of postage). They can be obtained from:

Island Publications, 132 Serpentine Road, Newtownabbey, Co. Antrim BT36 7JQ, Northern Ireland, UK.

1. **Life on the Interface** Belfast 'peaceline' community groups confront common issues.
2. **Sacrifice on the Somme** Ulster's 'cross-community' sacrifice in the First World War.
4. **Idle Hours** Belfast working-class poetry.
5. **Expecting the Future** A community play focusing on the effects of violence.
6. **Ulster's Shared Heritage** Exploring the cultural inheritance of the Ulster people.
7. **The Cruthin Controversy** A response to academic misrepresentation.
8. **Ulster's European Heritage** A celebration of Ulster's links with mainland Europe.
10. **The Battle of Moira** An adaptation of Sir Samuel Ferguson's epic poem *Congal.*
18. **At the Crossroads?** Further explorations by the Shankill Think Tank.
19. **Conflict Resolution** The missing element in the Northern Ireland peace process.
20. **Young People Speak Out** An exploration of the needs of Nationalist youth in Belfast.
21. **Puppets No More** An exploration of socio-economic issues by Protestant East Belfast.
22. **Beyond King Billy?** East Belfast Protestants explore cultural & identity-related issues.
23. **Are we not part of this city too?** Protestant working-class alienation in Derry.
24. **Orangeism and the Twelfth** Report of a cultural debate held in Protestant East Belfast.
25. **Broadening Horizons** The impact of international travel on attitudes and perceptions.
26. **Before the 'Troubles'** Senior citizens from Belfast's Shankill Road reminisce.
27. **Seeds of Hope** A joint exploration by Republican and Loyalist ex-prisoners.
28. **Towards a Community Charter** An exploration by the Falls Think Tank.
29. **Restoring Relationships** A community exploration of restorative justice.
30. **Separated by Partition** An encounter between Protestants from Donegal and Belfast.
31. **Left in Limbo** The experience of Republican prisoners' children.
32. **A question of 'community relations'** Protestants discuss community relations issues.
33. **Beyond Friendship** An exploration of the value of cross-border exchanges.
34. **Catalysts for change** A Los Angeles / Northern Ireland / Moldovan exchange.
35. **Dunmurry Reflections** Reminiscences from the 'outskirts'.
36. **Community relations: an elusive concept** An exploration by community activists.
37. **Living in a mixed community** The experience of Ballynafeigh, Ormeau Road.
38. **Cross-border reflections on 1916** Report of a cross-border conference.
39. **The forgotten victims** The victims' group H.U.R.T. reveal the legacy of 'The Troubles'.
40. **The unequal victims** Discussion by members of Loughgall Truth and Justice Campaign.
41. **Citizenship in a modern society** Report of a public debate.
42. **Whatever happened to the Peace Process?** Report of a public debate.
43. **Turf Lodge Reminiscences** Discussion by the members of Voices Women's Group.
44. **In search of a Haven** Discussion by members of HAVEN victims support group.
45. **An uncertain future** An exploration by Protestant community activists.
46. **The future of education** Views from North Belfast.
47. **Towards a cross-community charter** The Falls/Ballymacarrett Joint Think Tank.

The following titles are out of print, but can be supplied as laser copies (for same price):

3. **Ulster's Scottish Connection** Exploring the many links between Ulster and Scotland.
9. **Ulster's Protestant Working Class** A community exploration.
11. **Beyond the Fife and Drum** Belfast's Protestant Shankill Road debates the future.
12. **Belfast Community Economic Conference** Grassroots groups explore issues.
13. **A New Beginning** The Shankill Think Tank outlines its vision for the future.
14. **Reinforcing Powerlessness** Curtailing the voice of ordinary people.
15. **Ourselves Alone?** Belfast's Nationalist working class speak out.
17. **The Death of the Peace Process?** A survey of community perceptions.